Eight Ways to Lift Y[...]
and Live the Ultimate Life

RECHARGED

by
Christine Martin

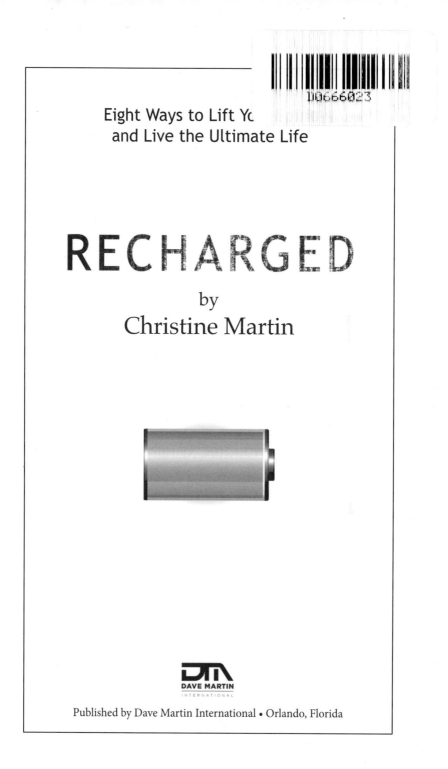

DM
DAVE MARTIN
INTERNATIONAL

Published by Dave Martin International • Orlando, Florida

15 14 13   11 10 9 8 7 6 5 4 3 2 1

RECHARGED
ISBN: 978-1-6284-734-1
Copyright © 2013 by Christine Martin

Published by:
Dave Martin International
P.O. Box 608150 Orlando, FL 32860

CONTENTS

INTRODUCTION
Why I Wrote This Book

Have you ever felt down and out? What a silly question! Of course, you have. With a title like RECHARGED: *Eight Ways to Lift Your Spirit, and Live the Ultimate Life,* you would not be reading this book if you didn't feel "down" sometimes. But I actually wrote this book because I have often felt "down" myself. Like any person, I have suffered through countless episodes of gloominess when I felt like the whole world had abandoned me. I have suffered through seasons when my zest for living was gone and when all the excitement of life had actually been siphoned from my body. I have even given up at times, feeling as if God himself had turned away from me and had given up on me.

More times than I can count, I remember finding a solitary place to cry, wondering when this lousy season of my life would be over. How long would this last? When would I get my breakthrough? Where was God? I felt like a little, lost girl in search of answers, but more importantly, in search of significance. And it was not until I finally realized some things that this depressing pattern finally ceased in my life. I realized, for instance, that God had never abandoned me. I realized that he was always there to guide me and to give me peace, even when I didn't know it. I realized that strength for the battle must come from deep within my own soul, from a realization that everything is going to be okay, that everything has a purpose, and that God will not allow anything to take place in my life that doesn't contribute to my overall wellbeing. And I realized that strength comes from the Lord.

Good news is something people want to share. When a girl finds an easy diet that really works or a great new store that sells designer shoes at half price, she wants to tell her friends about it. When a guy finds an investment that is earning him lots of money, he wants to share that information with his pals. I want to share my good news, too. After too many years of suffering through life's difficulties and after crying buckets of unnecessary tears, I have finally discovered how to live my everyday life in a way that can keep me in positive territory and keep my confidence level high, no matter what might be happening around me or to me. Because of the amazing truths in God's Word that I have discovered and applied, I now walk in a new assurance that, with God, all things are indeed possible and all things indeed work to my benefit.

It's hard sometimes. I'm not going to lie to you or stick my head in the sand like an ostrich and pretend that life is a continuous carousel of charismatic Christian exhilaration. In a world that can kick you hard and leave you wounded on the side of the road, it's difficult at times to keep your hopes high and your spirit elevated. But there are churches and friends that can help you finish the race. And more importantly, there are spiritual resources available to you that can help you lift your own spirit and motivate your own soul when nobody else is there.

Rushing through the endless chain of responsibilities and problems that each day presents can drain a woman's energy, increase her stress levels, and make her feel depleted of the mental and emotional nourishment she was created to possess. Then the occasional crisis can be added unexpectedly to actually put her over the edge. But with God's help, I have learned to relax, unwind, and soak up the potential for growth that these trials offer. I have learned to lift my own spirit to the place of internal peace that King David described in the 23rd Psalm when he wrote about God's ability to lead him beside the still waters and restore his soul. You, too, were created to be full of power, purpose, and potential. You, too, were created to be victorious and strong in your soul. But the choice is yours. It's not a matter of your circumstances; it's a matter of what you choose to do with them.

So I want to encourage you: Don't give up, because God can lift your spirit too, just as he lifted mine. No matter how "low" you might feel and no matter what may be weighing on you right now, you can learn the unchanging principles of God's Word that can enable you to soar above it all and to walk in victory and joy. Your desire for living can be revived, and your broken spirit can be restored. So if you have ever felt alone, discouraged, lost, without guidance, and without creativity... read on. This book was written just for you. And my prayer for you, as you begin this book, is that a newfound freedom will come over you, that the joy you have lost will be restored, and that your body, soul, and spirit will be lifted to new heights.

There lies within each and every one of us a God-given desire to survive the wounds we receive in the midst of life's battles. There lies within each of us a need to overcome, to win, and to triumph over those challenges that confront us and those enemies who oppose us. But when we come to believe that our wounds will not heal, that our sorrows will not cease, that our challenges cannot be overcome, or that our enemies cannot be defeated, the will to fight will slowly evaporate and the heart will begin to lose its strength.

In the pages that follow, however, you will learn how to regain what the enemy has stolen from you as your mind is filled with the thoughts and revelations that changed the way I approach my life, particularly the challenges of my life. So dive in with me; let's revisit the truths God has given us, and let's learn how to apply that wisdom. Stay with me, and stay focused.

HOW TO USE THE
WORKBOOK MODULES

Welcome to RECHARGED. Realizing that too many valuable books sit unused in libraries around the world, I have developed this companion guide to my book in the hope that you will use it to help you better understand and apply the life-changing truths presented in RECHARGED.

Before you begin using this helpful tool, I invite you to read through this brief introduction to the material so you can better understand how this workbook is designed and how to use it efficiently. But after you have familiarized yourself with the contents of this manual, you should start at the beginning and work systematically through the material as you read each chapter of the original book.

Be aware that the eight chapters of this workbook correspond with the eight chapters of the book and with the eight DVD video sessions that are included. Consequently, you should read through each chapter of the book and watch each corresponding video before you tackle the questions in the workbook, which are designed to stimulate your thinking and to help you relate the book's material to your everyday life. Each workbook module also includes an area to journal your feelings and insights as you learn how to implement the information you receive from the book and the videos.

EACH MODULE CONTAINS PROBING QUESTIONS AND ADDITIONAL EXERCISES LIKE…

- **Digging Deeper and Something to Think About** – thought-provoking exercises that will stimulate your thinking and increase your ability to remember the primary emphases of each chapter. These two sections of each module will help you practically apply the major teachings of the book.

- **Devotional** – a final thought from God's Word that will help drive home the focus of the chapter.

- **Prayer** – a prayer that the reader can utilize to jump-start his or her own prayer life in regards to the subject matter presented.

- **Food for Thought** – an expanded excerpt from Scripture that presents one or more of the prominent teachings of the chapter.

AND SCATTERED THROUGHOUT EACH MODULE
OF THE WORKBOOK, THE READER WILL FIND...

> • **Wisdom from Above** – verses quoted within the
> text of the original book.

> • **Could You Repeat That?** – memorable quotes ex-
> tracted from each chapter to help the reader remem-
> ber the key points that were made.

> • **In a Nutshell** – the quote from each chapter that
> best summarizes the main emphasis of the chapter.

For most of my adult life, I have been a teacher of God's Word. During my years of labor in God's kingdom, I have noticed that the vast majority of Christian people are people who are hungry for truth and hungry for wisdom. But I also have noticed another phenomenon in the church: I have noticed that many of these people buy books and DVDs only to place them on a shelf or inside a box and leave those things there unattended. Please don't let this happen to you.

You purchased this book because you were excited to learn how to lift your own spirit and to successfully navigate the challenges of life. So I encourage you to follow through with your hunger for knowledge. Invest some time in this valuable study. Information cannot serve its purpose if it sits idle on a bookshelf or inside a box in your attic. You must read it, study it, and apply it in order to grow.

But as you conscientiously engage the information I have presented here, you can do so with the absolute assurance that I will be praying for you. And I will be asking the Lord to give you success as you learn how to better handle life's inevitable problems. May you have good success and may the Lord be with you in this endeavor.

CHRISTINE MARTIN
August 2013

CHAPTER 1

Give It to God

In at least one respect, you and I are just alike. Over the course of my life, I have encountered many problems and countless unwelcomed situations that I was not equipped to handle. In the face of each of these challenges, I have had the opportunity to do things the right way by giving the problem to God or to do things the wrong way by internalizing the problem and attempting to solve it from a purely emotional posture. Over the span of my life, I have failed many times to give my problems to the Lord, and I have faced the consequences as a result of those poor decisions. But as time marches on, I am learning how to relinquish my challenges to God. I am learning how to bring God into the picture early in the problem-solving process, and I am learning to let God take care of those things I cannot control.

When I look back over my life, I sometimes roll my eyes and sigh when I stop to think about how ignorant I used to be regarding the proper way to deal with life's setbacks. But when I look back, I also am grateful that God has taught me some things along the way. None of my trials have been wasted, because all of them have played a role in helping me to understand what God wants me to do whenever a future problem intrudes upon my life.

One of the biggest things I have learned through many encounters with unwelcomed suffering is that God has appointed two schoolmasters to help me grasp the eternal principles of his kingdom. One of these teachers is kind and gentle; the other is harsh and cruel. Both of them are capable of teaching God's unchanging laws, but these two teachers use extremely different methods, and it is up to me to choose the instructor I want to utilize in any given situation.

I have to learn the lessons of life. As a child of God, I don't have the option of withdrawing from God's School of Christian Discipleship. When I surrendered my heart to Christ and told him that I wanted him to become the Lord of my life, he took me seriously and he immediately enrolled me in this lifelong "institute" of spiritual training and equipping. And he will not relent until he finishes the task of transforming me and I graduate with honors and heavenly awards.

So the assignment to follow Christ and to become more like him is not an option for me or any other Christian. I will be required to take the "classes" that God ordains for me in this mandatory school, and the Lord himself will select the order in which I take those classes. But I do have one option in this school of spiritual wisdom. I have the freedom to choose the instructor for each class I take. And the choice could not present a sharper contrast in teaching styles.

The first teacher is gentle and patient. She can be strong at times in the delivery of the information she imparts. But she is never cruel. She rarely hurts my feelings, and she is never overly forceful. Her name is Wisdom, and she is my favorite teacher. Ms. Wisdom imparts spiritual truth through academic methods. She introduces me to the principles of God's Word and explains to me how they work. Then she asks me to believe those principles and to practice them in my life. Ms. Wisdom instructs me through the Word of God by pointing out to me the many life lessons that the Bible contains. She instructs me also through the wise counsel of pastors, mentors, and successful people who have already journeyed where I desire to go. But even though her methods offer me the easier path through life, it is up to me to listen to her voice, to believe what she says, and to actually do what she tells me I should do. In other words, I have to trust that she is telling me the truth. I have to trust and apply the words of knowledge that she imparts.

But every time I fail to pass the test in Ms. Wisdom's class, I have to retake the same class with Mr. Reality. God, who enrolled me in this school of spiritual discipline the same day that I placed my life in his hands, prefers for me to learn the lessons of life from Ms. Wisdom, who always tells me the truth. But when I fail to listen to Ms. Wisdom or I fail to apply the things she teaches me, God then requires me to take the class again, and I find myself in the iron grip of a very different kind of teacher.

Unlike Ms. Wisdom, Mr. Reality doesn't teach with words, books, and chalkboards. He doesn't teach spiritual concepts and then release me to apply those concepts in my own life in my own way. Unlike Ms. Wisdom, Mr. Reality takes his students on a daily field trip. He teaches them through hands-on experience. He teaches them by thrusting them mercilessly into the real world, allowing them to learn the eternal truths they ignored in Ms. Wisdom's class by actually feeling the pain and consequences of their own foolish choices.

Mr. Reality's class is often referred to as "the School of Hard Knocks." He imparts wisdom experientially. He forces his students to learn the hard lessons of life by actually walking through them. For instance, there's a particular student in Mr. Reality's classroom right now who failed his class in marital faithfulness last year when he took that class under Ms. Wisdom. Ms. Wisdom pointed out to this man the fact that God has said, "Thou shalt not commit adultery" (Exodus 20:14, KJV). She also required the class to read several books about the painful experiences of those who failed to learn this lesson before it was too late. She brought in several lecturers who shared their personal stories about the sometimes-neglected consequences of disobeying this eternal law of God. Ms. Wisdom did everything she could do to help this man learn through mentoring and instruction that adultery is a bad thing and that it should be avoided at all costs.

But this particular student ignored everything Ms. Wisdom tried to teach him. He felt that he could enjoy the temporary pleasures of adultery and somehow escape the bitter consequences that all those guest lecturers, like King David, talked about in the class. He also felt that he was smart enough and that he possessed enough self-control to partake of adultery periodically while simultaneously avoiding its effects on his life. Only stupid people get caught, he thought to himself.

So this guy failed the class the first time around. He failed to get the message by reading the Bible. He failed to believe the message that was imparted to him by various teachers, lecturers, mentors, and counselors. Instead, he did his own thing and failed the test. And that's when God pulled him out of Ms. Wisdom's class and placed him in Mr. Reality's class. Now Mr. Reality takes him into the real world every day where he can personally experience the painful consequences of his actions. No more lectures! No more conceptual lessons from the Word of God! No more warnings and instruction! From this point on, Mr. Reality will teach this guy about adultery by letting him taste its bitter fruits. Mr. Reality will just stand there and let this guy be beaten up by life until he finally gets the point and passes the test. Then the student will be sent back to Ms. Wisdom's class to take her class on truthfulness. I wonder if he will listen this time.

With great appreciation to the Lord, I can say that I have learned a lot of life lessons by reading the Bible or by listening to my pastor or other spiritually mature people who have counseled me regarding the problems I have faced in life. With great appreciation to the Lord, I can say that I have made a lot of right choices in the face of great suffering. I have learned many of my lessons the easy way, and I have passed those tests. God has rewarded me accordingly.

Unfortunately, I also can say that I have failed a lot of tests. A whole lot of tests! Like you and like most people, there were a lot of lessons that I simply refused to learn in Ms. Wisdom's class. There were a lot of lessons I refused to learn from God and from other people. So like you, I have been forced to retake a lot of classes with Mr. Reality. I have been forced to learn through the harsh and bitter experiences of life those lessons that I refused to learn from God and from the many mentors he has placed in my life. And one of those vital life lessons that I learned the hard way was the lesson about handing things over to God. It took me a long time to learn to do that. Since God will not allow any student at SCD (the School of Christian Discipleship) to fail and since God requires students to retake classes until they finally pass them, God required me to learn this lesson over and over the hard way until I finally got the gist of what he was trying to teach me.

What was the lesson that God wanted me to grasp and incorporate into my daily life? What was the lesson that I had to take over and over before I eventually passed the final exam? It was the lesson that God wants me to stop carrying my problems around with me like a huge ball and chain, and he wants me to give those problems to him. He wants me to start living a life that is filled with peace and joy, not worry and frustration.

How about you? Have you learned this lesson yet? Probably not! If you had learned this lesson by now, this book wouldn't appeal to you. But the simple fact that you are reading this book tells me that you haven't yet learned how to give your problems to the Lord. So in a sincere effort to help you avoid learning this lesson the painful way in the School of Hard Knocks, let me tell you the same things that God and my spiritual mentors have tried to tell me throughout my life. Let me tell you what Ms. Wisdom used to tell me repeatedly when I was taking this class with her.

First of all, Ms. Wisdom read a lot of scriptures to me in an effort to help me see that God doesn't want me to carry my problems around with me. I especially remember 1 Peter 5:7, one of Ms. Wisdom's favorite verses on the subject. That passage of Scripture says, *"Give all your worries and cares to God, for he cares about you"* (NLT). She also frequently quoted Matthew 11:30. In fact, she used to have that verse of Scripture displayed on the wall of her classroom so the students could see it every day. That verse tells us that *"my yoke is easy and my burden is light."*

What I have learned since those early days in the School of Christian Discipleship is that God's people tend to make God's Word more complicated than it really is. We tend to muddy the waters with our own feet. In reality, the Bible is easy to understand. It says what it means, and it means what it says. In fact, I believe that the biggest problem with understanding and applying the Bible is not that the Bible is difficult to understand; the biggest problem for me is that the Bible is way too easy to understand. It hits me right where it hurts, and it hits me hard.

Secretly, we don't want the Bible to say what it says so clearly, because those clear teachings convict us and force us to see ourselves as we really are. So we make things more complicated than they need to be by changing the clear intent of the Scriptures to suit our needs and our circumstances. Consequently, we recite those positive, uplifting verses that tell us what we want to hear. But most of us don't want to deal with the parts of the Bible that challenge our thinking. Most of us would rather wait and learn the eternal truths of God the hard way at the School of Hard Knocks from Mr. Reality.

I have always found it ironic that a lot of Christian people can trust God to save their souls and they can trust God to resurrect their decaying bodies on a day in the distant future, but they simply cannot trust God to handle a comparatively small matter in their lives right now. Perhaps a person needs additional income. Perhaps a person needs God to intervene in his marriage. I find it ironic that, more often than not, this

Christian can believe God's promise to resurrect him from the dead on the day when the trumpet finally sounds, but he cannot trust God to provide him with a 15-percent pay raise or a revitalized marriage. So he worries, he frets, he panics, and he runs to the wrong people for advice and counsel. We humans, even the believers among us, are a strange breed indeed. It's just plain hard for us to learn to live according to the principles we profess and the tenets we claim to believe.

The fact is that God has told us to cast all our cares upon him. So if we say we believe God, we also should believe this promise. But most of us don't believe it in practical terms, and I didn't believe it either for a lot of years. Over time, however, when we refuse to give our problems to the Lord, negative consequences arise. We start living under stress, which affects our health. We start living under pressure, which affects our emotions. We start living under a cloud of worry and negativity, which affects our relationships. We start living under fear, and fear deprives us of joy, of potential, and of all our hopes and dreams. It also depletes our faith.

Actually, faith and fear are the same, if you really think about it. While faith is the inner confidence that good things are going to happen, fear is the inner confidence that bad things are going to happen. In reality, nothing has happened yet. But as you peer into the future and try to visualize the outcome of your current situation, you will either see a positive picture of your future (the result of faith) or you will see a negative picture of your future (the result of fear).

The Bible tells us that *"faith is the substance of things hoped for, the evidence of things not seen"* (Hebrews 11:1, KJV). Well, I suggest that fear is the same thing: Fear is the substance of things hoped for, the evidence of things not seen. Why is it, then, that most people can believe for the negative outcome, but not for the positive outcome? When the last chapter of their situation has not yet been written, why do most people lay out a plot within their own minds that takes them to the worst possible conclusion to their story rather than the best possible conclusion? But that's exactly what we do. It's human nature. It's the way sin has programmed us to think. We anticipate the worst. We expect the least favorable results. And I often fell victim to this universal mindset in my own life until the Holy Spirit finally got hold of me and taught me both the necessity and the methodology for turning my problems over to the Lord.

Man, in his fallen, sinful state, is preconditioned to anticipate the worst. So he talks to himself and convinces himself that the worst will occur. And when we talk to ourselves in negative terms all day long and then surround ourselves with others who bolster those negative feelings, we succumb to fear and depression.

"But Christine," you may ask. "What if I try to have a positive attitude and then my situation fails to turn out the way I want? What if I try to look on the bright side of things and then everything turns out bad anyway? That has happened to me before, so I'm naturally afraid to believe that everything is going to turn out positive in my life all the time."

My answer to your question is: So what if it does turn out a different way than you would like? What's the problem? There are so many things in life that you and I cannot control. So why worry about them? If you can do something to steer the ship of your life in the direction you want it to travel, then do something about your situation; don't just worry about it. But if you can't control the outcome of your own destiny, if the winds and waves of life are controlling your destiny for you and you cannot steer the ship in the direction you want to travel, then turn the ship over to God. What do you have to lose? Trust him. Maybe you wanted to sail to Hawaii and the storm took you to the Mediterranean instead. But what's so bad about that? If you release your situation to the Lord, I can tell you right now where you will end up. You will end up exactly where God wants you to end up. And if that's not the place you wanted to be, that's okay. Just trust the Lord. He has taken you there temporarily for a specific divine purpose. When he is finished, he will take you elsewhere. In the meantime, you won't die. Your problems are only temporary. So don't do permanent damage to yourself and others because of a temporary problem.

Our challenge as humans, and particularly as women, is that we allow our emotions to rule us. We find it difficult sometimes to release things to the Lord. We find it difficult to trust him. He might mess up our plans or rewrite the script to our lives that we have spent years outlining in our own minds.

But God showed me some time ago that this kind of mental struggle is unnecessary. He showed me that he has a plan for my life. And as long as I am not hindering God's will for my life through my own rebellious actions, nothing is going to happen in my life that is not approved by God or planned by God. And whether God causes it to happen or allows it to happen, everything that happens in my life is going to work to my benefit (see Romans 8:28).

Christians should make use of their problems, not run away from them. In fact, I have found that seasons of testing can end up becoming some of the most positive seasons of life when our attitudes are right. For instance, if I choose to lay my problems at the feet of Jesus instead of despising those problems and rebuking them and worrying about them, I get to see God's love demonstrated in my life in a new way. I get to see what the Lord can do.

Just think about that for a minute! Open your Bible to any place where a miracle is recorded, and then go back a few verses to find out how the recipients of that miracle were feeling just before God performed the miracle on their behalf. Were they worried? Were they afraid? Were they angry with God? Or did they give their problem to the Lord and trust him to intervene? Typically, you will find an attitude of faith among some and an attitude of fear among others.

When God parted the Red Sea, for instance, most of the people were in a state of panic. They looked in front of them, and there was the sea. They looked behind them, and there was the army of Egypt, sweeping down upon them to slaughter them all. They looked to the right and to the left, and there they found more Egyptian soldiers covering their escape routes. So they began to cry out and to blame Moses for their plight. But Moses refused to panic. He just gave the problem to God, and God found a solution to the problem. And believe me! Even though there were probably more than 2 million Jews there that day and thousands of Egyptian soldiers, not one person anticipated what God was about to do. Nobody except Moses expected the waters to part.

But how can you possibly know that God is able to part water until you have a problem in your life? Until you have a problem, you can never know his power, his love, or his level of commitment to you. So stop cursing your problems, and stop wilting in the presence of difficulties. Instead, accept life's challenges as a natural consequence of living in an imperfect world. Give them to the Lord. Ask him to take care of those parts of the problem you cannot resolve, and ask him to help you take care of the parts that you can resolve. Also ask him to let you soak up all the benefits that the trial was devised to bring to your life when he approved it.

A lot of times in my life, I have found that, even in the midst of chaos, I have gained strength, developed character, learned the tactics of the enemy, developed faith, and nurtured newfound qualities like patience and persistence. I also have developed a more accurate understanding of the temporal nature of life and a deeper realization of how life is supposed to be in this present world. And I have come to better understand the Lord and how he works in our lives.

I do believe that God allows bad things to happen in the life of the believer. I don't believe that God makes those things happen, but I do believe that he allows them. However, I don't believe that the majority of life's problems flow from God or even from Satan. I believe that most of life's problems flow either from the natural conflicts that arise between imperfect people as a result of their competing interests or from our own self-inflicted wounds. More often than not, the big problems we face in life are problems we create for ourselves through our own choices or actions. But even though God is gracious and forgiving, we tend to double-down on our mistakes. We tend to make our problems worse by the way we react to them. We overreact. Driven by emotions, especially fear, we take a small problem and make it bigger than it really is.

Allow me to demonstrate: Right now, I would like you to think about one of the biggest problems you ever faced. Pick something that is behind you, a problem that has already been resolved, so that intense emotions will not arise when you think about it. Now I want you to tell me the exact date when that problem arose in your life. You can't remember the exact date, can you? I rest my case.

At the time when that problem was occurring, everything else in your life ceased. You were fixated on that problem, and nothing else mattered. You couldn't eat. You couldn't sleep. You were physically present at work, but you weren't really there (if you know what I mean). That problem absolutely consumed you every minute of every day until it was finally resolved. But in hindsight, you can't even remember the date.

In fact, you can't remember most of the details of that problem now that the problem has passed. The problem didn't kill you, and now that it has worked itself out, you realize that it wasn't as big of a problem as you thought at the time. But while you were in the midst of the storm, you magnified it in your heart and mind until it became bigger than life.

Here's the point: Even though the problem may now be a thing of the past, there was a lesson that God wanted you to learn in the midst of the storm. He wanted you to learn to release that problem to him and to walk in faith, not fear. Did you do that in the heat of the battle, or did you simply push through the problem the same way you push through all the rest of your problems in life? If you failed to learn the spiritual lesson that God was trying to teach you, he will just have to send you back to Mr. Reality's classroom to repeat that course.

God allows his children to face obstacles so they can learn the reliability of God's promises. Even in the midst of a great challenge, God never abandons his children. He never forsakes them. And he eventually brings them through. In fact, he brings them through triumphantly. And along the way, he develops faith in their hearts and character in their souls. He makes us better people and better disciples by allowing us to navigate the great storms of life.

If we become better as a result of our conflicts, God moves us along to the next level of spiritual growth. But if we become bitter as a result of our conflicts, we will be forced to repeat the class. If we become joyful even when things are difficult, God promotes us. But if we become angry, we must go back and learn what we failed to learn the first time. If we become forgiving, we graduate from that particular class and move up to the accelerated level. But if we become hurt and display our wounds for the whole world to see, we will just have to get back on that bus and go back on that same field trip with Mr. Reality until we finally learn the lesson we need to learn. We are in this school of discipleship for life, and God is in no hurry. As long as it takes, he will keep teaching us, first in Ms. Wisdom's class and then, if necessary, in Mr. Reality's class until we finally get the point. It's up to you and it's up to me how we choose to complete the educational requirements that God has set before us.

You and I have a choice, therefore. God will never deviate from his divine plan to rebuild us in the image of his Son, but you and I always have the freedom to choose how we will complete the course of study. We can do it the easy way, or we can do it the hard way. We can learn early, or we can learn late. We can take the shortcut, or we can take the long and winding road. We can learn from Ms. Wisdom, or we can learn from Mr. Reality. We can choose "life," or we can choose "death."

And just in case that decision becomes too hard for us to make, God has given us a little hint regarding the better choice. He has told us to "choose life" (Deuteronomy 30:19). But when it comes to the problems of life, the way to choose "life" is by giving that problem to the Lord and by continuing to walk in his joy. A person chooses "death" by dragging his problems around with him until all the areas of his life are negatively affected. A person chooses "death" by filling his heart with fear, filling his mind with doubt, filling his mouth with negative words that nobody wants to hear, and filling his marriage and the other important relationships of his life with tension, friction, and outright conflict. A person who ignores the wisdom of God and the counsel of God in favor of his own pathway through life's difficulties is the person whose negative attitudes will eventually create "death" in every aspect of his existence.

So choose "life." Choose to do the right thing in the right way. But just as important, choose to do the right thing in the right way with the right attitude, because, in the end, it's not the trials and tribulations that will enable you to draw closer to God; it's the way you choose to endure those trials and tribulations that will most powerfully affect your life, your relationships, and your spiritual health. It's the attitudes that come out of those seasons of testing that will endure. In the face of such challenges, you can choose an attitude of "life" by giving your problems to God, by allowing him to deal with the substance of your difficulties, and by allowing him to settle the score with those who violated you in some way. You can choose "life" by giving your problems to God and by allowing him to become your strength, your hope, your peace, and your comforter. So trust him. Let him have his way in your life. Let him be Lord. He has your best interests in mind.

At times, a person can become his own worst enemy. Yes, people can be downright mean sometimes, even cruel. And yes, circumstances can sometimes be unfair and extremely brutal. But most of the really big and really damaging problems that you will face in your lifetime will be those problems you created for yourself in response to a smaller, more manageable problem that you refused to surrender to God. Your reactions to a small problem can often create a bigger problem because of the decisions you make in the heat of confusion, the words you speak in the heat of a battle, or the changes you make in the heat of a moment created by a small, temporary problem. Your spiritual life also is shaped in these moments of testing. The way that you respond to life's challenges will either make you bitter or better, depending on the choices you make. And the way you deal with people in the midst of life's challenges will either mark you as a "good" person or a "bad" person among those who know you.

So when life hands you a pile of sour grapes, just do the following four things:

1. REST. Stop placing blame. Stop trying to pin your problems on God, on other people, or even on yourself. Stop finding fault. In fact, stop everything and ask God to show you how you should handle the problem from your end while he takes care of the things you cannot control. Also ask him to help you navigate the problem in a way that will demonstrate your faith to everyone who is watching you.

2. REGROUP. Take time to breathe and think. Some problems need urgent attention. If you find a member of your family unconscious on the bathroom floor, you don't need to pray about that situation. Just call an ambulance. But the vast majority of our problems should not be addressed with a knee jerk reaction. Instead, we should think and pray (even fast). We should ask God to gently and systematically walk us through the problem one step at a time until the problem is resolved.

3. RELAX. Put your emotions on hold. The first response of the average person to any unforeseen challenge is almost always an emotional response. Sudden trauma of any type triggers a chemical response in the brain that releases all kinds of hormones in major doses. We are inclined, therefore, to make decisions that are based on internal chemical overloads rather than rational thinking or purposeful faith. If the problem is not urgent (like the unconscious family member), then make yourself take a deep breath and relax, and make yourself wait on God for an answer. If you do, the Holy Spirit will take over.

4. RETREAT. Before you do anything or say anything, find a solitary place where you can pray, and then seek the Lord regarding your problem. If you need to "vent," this is the time to let it all hang out. Don't worry! God can take it. In fact, he already knows how you feel anyway, so you might as well put it all on the table—everything you are feeling and everything you are thinking. As you do, you will find that God will take these weighty things off you and take them upon himself. You also will find that God will start working right away to guide you through your dilemma.

Jesus is eager to deliver you and to rescue you. He is eager to perform a miracle, if necessary, to guide you victoriously through your problem. But the Lord is much more interested in teaching you how to surrender to him. This is the real lesson he wants to impart through every trial he allows in your life.

Your heart belongs to the Lord, so let the Lord mend it and let him provide you with answers as you relinquish to him the reins of your life. Let him decide when and where and how he will resolve the difficulties in your life. I know this isn't easy. I know from my own personal experience how hard this can be. It's human nature to want to understand why bad things happen to us, and it's human nature for us to seek revenge on those who deliberately contribute to our pain. And it's human nature to blame ourselves for many of our own problems. Nevertheless, while a thorough postmortem of the problem can sometimes help us understand how the problem occurred, no problem is ever solved by assigning blame or seeking revenge. Everything is gained by learning to surrender to the Lord.

Jesus said, *"Do to others what you would have them do to you"* (Matthew 7:12). So the law of God's kingdom is to take the initiative and to treat other people the way we would like for them to treat us. The law of God's kingdom is to plant seeds of kindness and seeds of appropriate behavior, regardless of whether those seeds give us an immediate return on our investment.

But the law of the world is exactly the opposite. The law of the world is to respond in kind whenever someone offends us or harms us in some way. We naturally do unto others what they have already done unto us. We naturally speak about others as they have spoken about us. And we naturally demonstrate the same attitude toward others that they have demonstrated toward us. The "flesh" of man is retaliatory, not creative. It is vengeful, not forgiving; responsive, not proactive. When our hearts have been wounded, we seek retribution. When our reputations have been damaged, we seek retaliation. When our egos have been bruised, we seek to get even. And we have great difficulty surrendering such things to a God we cannot see.

But the law of the kingdom of God is a law of personal surrender toward God and a law of mandatory forgiveness toward others. We cannot live under God's favor and we cannot maintain spiritual intimacy with the Lord as long as we refuse to surrender our hearts to him and as long as we insist on solving our problems our own way.

There's a funny little elevator in the kingdom of God. If you want to go up, you have to press the "down" button. And if you want to go down, you have to press the "up" button. In other words, to get where you want to go in the kingdom of God, you often have to do the exact opposite of what human nature teaches you to do. To become the greatest, for instance, you have to become the least (see Luke 22:26). To become the leader, you have to become the servant (see Matthew 20:27). If you want to receive, you have to give (see Luke 6:38). And if you want to live in the Spirit, you have to die to the flesh (see Romans 8:13).

So, if you want an answer to the problem that haunts you, you have to be content with no answer right now. If you want to win the battle you are fighting, you have to surrender your heart to the Lord. And if you want victory, you have to give up and let God fight your battles for you. You have to release to him every conflict, every challenge, every setback, and every temporary defeat. You have to trust him, and you can only learn to trust him by actually trusting him.

I can clearly remember a time in my life when I had

been betrayed very badly, and all I wanted to do was defend myself. I wanted everyone to know who was really at fault in this situation, and I wanted everyone to know that I was pure in the matter. But this was one of those occasions when I was desperately trying to practice what I preach, a time when I was doing everything in my power to release the situation to God.

To this day, the truth has never come out. It never became obvious to those who were watching from the sidelines who was guilty and who was innocent in this matter. And the way things look right now, the truth may never come out. But I don't care anymore, because I have given the problem to the Lord. God knows the truth, so, in his time and in his way, he will vindicate me in the matter. Until then, the internal knowledge that I have done everything right in this situation is a great source of comfort to me. I have refused to defend myself by lashing out at others. I have refused to try to convince all the onlookers that they should be on my "team" and support me in my conflict with the other person. I am maturing spiritually, and that makes me feel good about my future destiny in Christ.

Surrendering this difficult situation to the Lord has also taught me that I can survive a problem without resorting to "carnal" methods. I can do the right thing and feel good about it. I can do the right thing and walk out of the battle unscathed. I can learn to actually love my enemies and to pray for them even while I face the reality of what they have done to me. I can learn to forgive.

Did the situation hurt me? Oh, yeah, in many different ways! But it helped me to see myself clearly. It helped me to recognize my own weaknesses and to identify my own strengths. This painful trial also taught me to distinguish between my real friends and those fair-weather friends who were only hanging around because of the things I could do for them or the things I could add to their lives. And the wealth of experience I gained in this situation helped me to realize that Jesus is indeed "closer than a brother" (Proverbs 18:24) and that he is able to heal a broken heart while simultaneously carrying his wounded child through the problem to the other side. We can never know what God is capable of doing until we find ourselves in a situation we cannot handle alone and step back to watch what he does to address the situation on our behalf.

Humans are an interesting and complicated species. We are amazing in so many ways. But one of the most interesting things about people is that all of us know the truth deep down inside. We know what we ought to do in the face of conflict or in the presence of disappointment or outright devastation in our lives. We know we should give these things to the Lord and surrender our hearts to him in these kinds of situations. We know that tribulations will come, no matter how spiritually minded we may be (see John 16:33). And we know that the only thing we can truly control whenever life starts spinning out of control is our own response to the challenge.

If a child of God refuses to submit his problem to the Lord whenever a trial arises in his life, that believer will soon discover that nothing is gained when God is excluded from the formula. Like every other human being on this planet, the believer must occasionally endure episodes of suffering. In those times, panic and conflict won't make the problem any better. The believer must learn that refusing to give his dilemma to the Lord can only result in the hardening of his own heart and can actually compound his problem further. Worry and unbelief can never make things better.

So people should surrender to the Lord in such matters. And when a child of God surrenders himself to Christ, especially in the midst of a raging storm, he will find that his trial actually works to his benefit. The journey through that trial can actually build his faith and change him in many positive ways. Like the person who fails to submit to God, the faithful man or woman of God will still be required to navigate many storms. But the faithful person knows that God can do some incredibly amazing things when we take a step back and release our problems to him. The faithful person also knows that the right attitude in the midst of the storm means inevitable victory over the storm and positive changes in his or her life.

So give it to God. It's about time that you try a new approach to life's most difficult battles. It's about time that you try faith instead of fear and peace instead of panic. It's about time that you give God an opportunity to do something truly amazing in your life and your circumstances.

When life becomes really hard and the future looks really bleak, don't struggle, don't fret, and don't try to cope with your problem alone. Put your situation in the hands of the Lord. Trust that he knows what is best for you and for everyone else involved with you in the battle. Quit making excuses, and quit waiting until the next time to do what you know you need to do. Just take a deep breath and hand the thing to God. Believe me, he will know what to do about the situation. And when he does his thing in his way and in his time, your faith will be enhanced, your life will be changed, and your circumstances will be altered forever. When God touches a difficult situation, it can never be the same. And when God takes your heart in his hands, it can never feel the same.

MODULE 1

GIVE IT TO GOD

Please refer to Chapter 1 in Christine Martin's book, RE-CHARGED, and to Session 1 of the teaching series before starting work on this module.

GIVE IT TO GOD

1. Can you recall a difficult situation in your life where you refused to give the problem to God and instead approached the problem from a purely intellectual perspective? What happened? What did you learn from this experience?

_____

_____

_____

2. Do you trust God to save your soul from the penalty of death that awaits all unbelievers? Do you believe that God will resurrect your body after you die? Do you trust him to solve your everyday problems?

_____

_____

3. Do you typically obey the words of Jesus by casting all your cares upon him, or do you normally bear the weight of your problems and challenges?

_____

_____

_____

4. Can you recall a difficult time in your life when unforeseen circumstances took you in a direction you did not want to travel? What happened? How did things work out? What good things occurred as a result of this "detour" in your life?

_____

_____

_____

5. Christine Martin explains that God will take care of the parts of our problems that we cannot control, but God expects us to take care of those parts of the problem that we are able to control. Give an example of a problem in your life that required joint participation between you and the Lord. What part did you do to solve your own problem? What role did God play in solving the problem?

_____

_____

_____

6. Can you recall a problem in your life that you made worse by the way you reacted to the problem? What hap-

pened? What role did your emotions play in the situation?

_____

_____

_____

7. Can you remember a difficult situation in your life when the presence of God became more "real" to you as a result of the challenge? Explain.

_____

_____

_____

8. Can you recall a time in your life when your inappropriate response to a problem created additional problems for you? Describe what happened.

_____

_____

_____

9. When a particularly challenging problem comes your way, are you typically disappointed when the best possible outcome fails to materialize or are you typically surprised when the worst possible outcome fails to occur? In other words, do you normally approach the problem with expectations of a positive result or expectations of a negative result?

_____

_____

_____

10. Describe a situation you have faced that helped you distinguish your true friends from your fair-weather friends. What other good results did God produce from you from this bad situation?

_____

_____

_____

DIGGING DEEPER

Christine Martin used the analogy of two very different teachers to illustrate the two very different ways that God teaches us the eternal principles of his kingdom. The first teacher is Ms. Wisdom, who imparts knowledge through instruction and counsel. The second teacher is Mr. Reality, who imparts knowledge through the harsh and bitter experiences of life.

Give an example of a significant life lesson that you learned at the hands of Ms. Wisdom. Explain how you learned this lesson and why you consider yourself fortunate that you did not have to learn the lesson in the "School of Hard Knocks."

_____

_____

_____

Give an example of a significant life lesson that you were forced to learn the hard way, at the hands of Mr. Reality. Explain why it would have been better for you to learn the lesson through the wise counsel of God and others.

_____

_____

_____

A PROMISE WORTH REMEMBERING

I have told you these things, so that in me you
may have peace. In this world you will have trouble.
But take heart! I have overcome the world.
John 16:33

Many Christians come to the Lord with a false expectation of life. Yes, there are many wonderful things we can expect from the Lord. As Christians, we can expect his presence to be with us at all times and in all situations. As Christians, we can expect his Holy Spirit to guide us and to comfort us in our battles. We can expect the Lord to perform miracles in our lives when those miracles are appropriate. We can expect his favor and his goodness to shine upon us as we follow him obediently through life.

But God never promised us that life would always be smooth sailing. In fact, he promised us the exact opposite. He promised us that we would be tempted by the tempter. He promised us that we would be persecuted for our faith. He also promised us that "in this world you will have trouble." So if you like to quote the promises of God or post them on your refrigerator door, here's one that you might want to remember.

Many people believe that the Christian life is an easy life and that the sinner's life is a hard life. But this outlook on life is too simplistic. Life just doesn't work that way. Sometimes life can be cruel. Sometimes life can be harsh. Sometimes life can be unfair to believers and unbelievers alike. Sometimes storms can arise as the waves fill our boats with water and the winds blow us off course.

Jesus himself warned us that we should expect to be challenged by life. But Jesus also told us to "take heart." He reminded us that he has "overcome the world." So the next time you find yourself in peril on the high seas of life, be prudent and be diligent. Do what you can do to keep your boat afloat and to keep yourself on course. But trust the "captain of your soul" to lead you through the storm to safety on the other side.

SOMETHING TO THINK ABOUT

Negative consequences can occur whenever we internalize our problems. God did not design human beings to carry the weight of life's troubles without his help. So when we refuse to relinquish our problems to the Lord, we can often make the problems worse. In addition, there can be consequences in other areas of our lives.

One of the primary residual consequences associated with life's challenges is the increase in stress. In recent years, medical researchers have made a direct connection between heightened stress levels and disease. How have the unresolved problems in your life affected your stress levels? What can you do to rectify this problem?

Stress can also have an adverse effect on a person's emotional health and wellbeing. Have you ever seen evidence of emotional instability in your life that can be directly linked to an ongoing problem or challenge?

A cloud of worry or negativity can also impact one's relationships. Have you ever noticed yourself responding differently to the significant people in your life due to the presence of a difficult problem? How do your problems affect your relationships with the people you know and love?

MY PRAYER OF SURRENDER

Father, I know in my heart that I should give my problems to you. But that is hard to do. Please forgive me for not trusting you in the past, and please help me to trust you with my problems in the future. Also teach me to know the difference between those things I should release to you and those things that require my personal attention and effort. I want to be an aggressive problem-solver, but I don't want to wear myself out trying to take your place, and I don't want to make my problems worse by holding onto them and reacting to them in an inappropriate way. When I face my next trial in life—my next opportunity to grow spiritually—help me to take a deep breath and release the situation to you. Then help me to rest in you and trust you to do the right thing in the right way at the right time. In Jesus' name, Amen!

MY SPIRITUAL JOURNAL

Take a few moments to record your thoughts regarding this week's session on giving your problems to the Lord. What new things did you learn? What new insights and revelations have you had? What life-changing truths did Christine Martin impart that have impacted your thinking? What changes will you make in the days ahead?

_____

_____

_____

FOOD FOR THOUGHT

The Bible describes God's Words as spiritual bread and spiritual meat. It is designed to nourish the spirit and the soul in the same way that food nourishes the body. So read the following scripture every day this week, repeating it out loud when you read it, and memorize it, if possible. And while you meditate upon this passage, make notes about anything you may observe about your personal life and any changes you may want to make.

This day I call the heavens and the earth as witnesses against you that I have set before you life and death, blessings and curses. Now choose life, so that you and your children may live and that you may love the Lord your God, listen to his voice, and hold fast to him. For the Lord is your life, and he will give you many years in the land he swore to give to your fathers, Abraham, Isaac and Jacob.
Deuteronomy 30:19-20

_____

_____

_____

WISDOM FROM ABOVE

Come to me, all you who are weary and burdened, and I will give you rest. Take my yoke upon you and learn from me, for I am gentle and humble in heart, and you will find

*rest for our souls. For my yoke is easy
and my burden is light.*
Matthew 11:28-30

*And we know that in all things God works for
the good of those who love him, who have
been called according to his purpose.*
Romans 8:28

*Give all your worries and cares to God,
for he cares about you.*
I Peter 5:7 (NLT)

COULD YOU REPEAT THAT?

God wants me to stop carrying my problems around with me like a huge ball and chain, and he wants me to give those problems to him.

As you peer into the future and try to visualize the outcome of your current situation, you will either see a positive picture of your future (the result of faith) or you will see a negative picture of your future (the result of fear).

The only thing we can truly control whenever life starts spinning out of control is our own response to the challenge.

IN A NUTSHELL

We can never know what God is capable of doing until we find ourselves in a situation we cannot handle alone.

CHAPTER 2

When I Know, I Grow

With knowledge comes responsibility, and with responsibility we need wisdom. With wisdom comes success, and with success we achieve our goals, find purpose for our lives, and experience the happiness that God created us to know. Wisdom, therefore, is a proven pathway to joy. It is one of God's most preferred mechanisms for elevating a person's spirit and enhancing his or her self-worth.

In fact, wisdom is the most important quality for success in life. With it, all other virtues can be acquired. Without it, no other virtues really matter. According to the Bible, wisdom will "keep" you as long as you follow her instructions (Proverbs 4:6, ESV). She will "rebuke" you when you go astray (Proverbs 1:23). She will "enter your heart" when you need her the most (Proverbs 2:10). She will "save you" when troubles threaten (Proverbs 2:12). Wisdom will "prolong your life" (Proverbs 3:2), "bring you prosperity" (Proverbs 3:2), "win you favor and a good name in the sight of God and man" (Proverbs 3:4), and "make your paths straight" (Proverbs 3:6).

Wisdom will increase your confidence and strengthen your resolve. Wisdom will undergird your life with focus and your relationships with substance. Wisdom will elevate your soul. Because wisdom fortifies every aspect of your life and sets everything in your life on a firm foundation, wisdom can definitely impact the quality of your life and can definitely affect the state of your mind. Wisdom can also give you patience when endurance is required and motivation when action is needed. Nothing can stabilize your heart and your daily life quite like wisdom.

If you make business deals, wisdom is essential. If you invest in mutual funds or real estate, wisdom is necessary. If you run a household or raise children, wisdom is vital. If you serve at your church, entertain guests, or collaborate with others in a common cause, wisdom is fundamental to the success of your life and the happiness of your heart. It should be applied to every decision we make and every act we perform.

In fact, through the prophet Hosea, God strongly emphasized the necessity of wisdom when he said, "My people are destroyed from lack of knowledge" (Hosea 4:6). Sometimes we Christians believe that God is not going to allow us to suffer in any way. Sometimes we believe that God is always going to protect us from life's pains and shelter us from life's storms. And it is true that God will fight our battles for us when we are viciously attacked and vindicate us when we are wrongly accused. But God will not reward stupidity. In fact, the entire book of Proverbs was written to drive home this point: If you make wise decisions, you will be rewarded accordingly, but if you consistently make foolish decisions, you will face the consequences of your own uninformed choices.

So God will protect you from the enemy, but he won't always protect you from yourself. Sometimes, the only way he can teach us the difference between right and wrong is to let us taste the fruits of our own actions and drink the wine of our own ignorance. Through life itself, God reminds us every day that wisdom is essential and that we should value it and pursue it with all our might.

Christian people are not immune to the pains of life, particularly the self-inflicted pains that result from unwise actions. Without wisdom, therefore, even "my people" can be destroyed. Even the strongest and most committed believers can be negatively affected if they reject knowledge and despise wisdom. Consequently, wisdom is exalted in the Word of God, and the lifelong pursuit of knowledge is highly encouraged. In fact, it is commanded.

But the good news is that God has promised to impart wisdom to those who realize that they lack it and who cherish its value for their lives. Through James, God has said, "If any of you lacks wisdom, you should ask God, who gives generously to all without finding fault, and it will be given to you" (James 1:5). Consequently, one of the most reliable things you can do to lift your spirit and elevate your own soul is to pursue wisdom for your life. But if you lack the wisdom you desire, God has promised to infuse your life with his wisdom, provided you come to a place where you understand its value and cherish its benefits enough that you are prompted to request it in prayer.

The New Testament word for wisdom is the Greek word sophia. To have this sophia kind of wisdom is to have the heart and mind of God. To have the heart and mind of God is to think like him and act like him. This kind of wisdom leads to success in everything we engage. It leads to fulfillment, significance, happiness, and a sense of purpose. But no man, no woman is going to ask for this kind of wisdom unless he or she appreciates its value. So when a person comes to the point where he cares enough about the riches of wisdom and the benefits that knowledge can provide, that person will start seeking God for the wisdom that he realizes he needs. And God will respond by liberally providing that wisdom to the one who requests it.

When people pray, they always pray about the things they love or value. So the man who cares enough about wisdom to start requesting it in prayer is the man who will care enough about it to pursue it, embrace it, and place great value upon it. He is the man who will follow the advice of Solomon by seeking after wisdom.

There are certain behaviors that separate children from adults. If you have children, you will recognize these distinguishing traits. A child, for instance, likes to play with toys. But adults like "toys" too. You can tell the difference between a child and an adult by how much they spend on their toys and how much time they invest in taking care of their toys.

Another thing that distinguishes children from adults is their attitude toward sleep. Children cry because they have to go to bed early; adults cry because they can't go to bed early. A child cries when he is told that he must take a midday nap; an adult rejoices when he is told that he can take a midday nap.

But a more serious distinction between children and adults is the difference between the things they value. You can probably testify along with me that, as a person grows older, that person tends to place increasing value and increasing significance on the simpler things of life. When we are young, we tend to overlook the value of life's simplest and most fundamental things. We tend to take them for granted. As we mature, however, we eventually come to realize that it is the fundamental things of life that give life its purpose and lace it with delight.

Sometimes a person can live his entire life without acquiring a functional level of wisdom and understanding. But those who do obtain wisdom tend to garner it later in life rather than earlier. As the years go by, wisdom increases. That's the natural flow of life. Why? Because wisdom is usually acquired from experience, and experience comes from tackling the difficult issues of life. With the passage of time, therefore, people tend to place more value on the things that truly matter. They tend to develop a more positive outlook on the fundamental elements of their existence. But nowhere is it written in stone that a man must be old to be wise, and nowhere is it commanded that a woman must wait until the latter years of her life to acquire knowledge. Wisdom is available to all who seek it. Unfortunately, most people tend to seek it later rather than sooner. They tend to wait until all other options have failed before embracing the quality of wisdom.

But with wisdom comes a natural ease about things, a joy derived from life's simplest pleasures, and an elevated spirit that is content and at peace. Wisdom tends to bring its own unique form of happiness because of the sense of satisfaction and success that accompanies it.

The things you know help you grow. The knowledge you possess shapes you and makes you the person you are. Obviously, you can never rise above the level of wisdom you have achieved. Neither can you act upon information you do not possess. But wisdom is the ability to command the knowledge you do possess. It is the quality of utilizing the information you have at your disposal.

Wisdom, therefore, is simple. At the same time, it is profound because the person who draws upon less information with wisdom will typically surpass the person who stores away greater quantities of information yet lacks the ability to apply it to his life. In fact, this distinction is often seen in casual social conversation. Have you ever attended a party or a social event where people shared spontaneous conversation about politics, sports, current events, or popular culture? Typically, the person who says the most speaks from a vast reservoir of knowledge. But quite often, the person who speaks the least says the most profound and memorable things.

Foolishness is often exhibited through a lot of chatter that really carries no weight, while wisdom is often expressed through a timely sentence expertly uttered. Foolishness also creates confusion, but wisdom solves a lingering problem or puts to rest a nagging sense of uncertainty. Foolishness is obvious, but wisdom is discreet.

In fact, the oft-quoted thirty-first chapter of Proverbs, which describes the virtuous woman, tells us that this model of feminine strength *speaks with wisdom, and faithful instruction is on her tongue*" (Proverbs 31:26). The classic woman of God, therefore, is wise. She speaks with intelligence and cleverness. She is cultured in mind and social graces. She is strong in spirit and in heart. She is not one given to profuse speech, but when she does speak, her words serve a purpose. They communicate life, and they impart "instruction."

In this verse, wisdom is directly linked to the mind, because "instruction" is a word that refers to the mental capabilities of man. Wisdom, therefore, is expressed through the

tongue, but it performs its work within the mind. And this
reminds us of God's primary interest in the human mind.
God is primarily interested in "renewing" it; he is not interested in enhancing it. In spite of what some may believe, God
is not interested in advancing the human mind. He is not
interested in perfecting it. He is not interested in nurturing
it or improving it. According to the Bible, God is only interested in "renewing" the mind of man.

The apostle Paul said, *"Be transformed by the renewing
of your mind. Then you will be able to test and approve what
God's will is—his good, pleasing and perfect will"* (Romans
12:2). And the New Living Translation translates that verse
this way: *"Let God transform you into a new person by changing the way you think. Then you will learn to know God's will
for you, which is good and pleasing and perfect."*

God doesn't want to "fix" your mind. He doesn't want to
"repair" your mind. He doesn't want to "expand" your mind
or "broaden" your mind. He doesn't even want to "restore"
your mind. God wants to "transform" your mind. He wants
to "renew" your mind completely. He wants to eradicate the
way of thinking that was ingrained in you by the world, and
he wants to completely alter the way you see him, the way
you see yourself, the way you see others, and the way you see
life and eternity. He wants to permeate your thinking with
sound, reliable, biblically based wisdom, which is "perfect"
and "pleasing" and "good." He wants to lift your spirit and
give you a firm grip on your own nature by renewing your

mind with wisdom.

Some people are confused and defeated because they lack wisdom and understanding about themselves and their situations. Many people believe that they evolved from monkeys. Many others believe that their fate is determined by the alignment of the planets. And still others believe that they are entirely alone in the universe. They see themselves as "victims" of life and of social and political institutions they cannot control.

But knowledge is power, so the right application of knowledge leads to success. The person with the mind of God knows that his supernatural origins at the hands of a loving God point to a supernatural destiny that rests in the hands of that God. And the person with the mind of God knows that while people and circumstances may constantly change around him, bringing unforeseen challenges to his life every day, the things that truly matter will never change. God's Word is sure; God's promises are fixed.

Wisdom "is more profitable than silver and yields better returns than gold" (Proverbs 3:14). *Wisdom "is more precious than rubies"* (Proverbs 3:15). But without wisdom, silver and gold and rubies can only bring problems and pain, because "things" by themselves are a leading source of heartache and they often yield more sorrow than happiness. They definitely consume our time and require our attention. But that which is produced and managed through wisdom typically brings success and great contentment.

Without wisdom, good "things" can definitely be obtained, but these things will usually bring many problems with them. With wisdom, however, things will come into one's life in God's time and in God's way and will lead to blessing rather than sorrow, because the man with knowledge will know how to manage his things and not allow his things to manage him.

The little book of James is one of my favorite books in the Bible. It is short, but direct. Because of the book's practical teachings and its references to wisdom, many people have referred to James as the "New Testament book of Proverbs." Regarding wisdom, James wrote, *"But the wisdom that comes from heaven is first of all pure; then peace-loving, considerate, submissive, full of mercy and good fruit, impartial and sincere"* (James 3:17). So James has given us the seven proven qualities of divine wisdom to help us understand its worth.

First, true wisdom, the wisdom that comes from heaven, is pure. This means that it is not mixed or contaminated with any other substance. When we refer to "pure gold," for instance, we are referring to the uncompromised element. Pure gold has no other component. The same is true of "pure silver" or "pure sugar." God wants all of us to be pure. In other words, he wants us to be focused on him and his ways. He will never be content with a tainted heart that is partially committed to him yet polluted with other purposes and affections. He wants all of you. He wants all of me.

Jesus reminded us that the greatest commandment is to *"love the Lord your God with all your heart and with all your soul and with all your mind"* (Matthew 22:37). God won't share our hearts or our devotion. According to the Old Testament, he is "a jealous God" (Exodus 20:5; Deuteronomy 4:24). He broods over you with a godly jealousy, and he wants all your heart, soul, mind, and strength. But the good news is that the pure in heart are blessed. They are blessed because "they will see God" (Matthew 5:8).

If the heart is pure, the mind is at ease. If the heart is pure, the soul is calm. If the heart is pure, the attitudes of the one who possesses that pure heart will always be positive and life will be more rewarding and less problematic.

Second, genuine wisdom is peace-loving. The writer of Hebrews said, *"Make every effort to live in peace with all men"* (Hebrews 12:14). In addition, Jesus said, *"Blessed are the peacemakers: for they shall be called the children of God"* (Matthew 5:9, KJV). And the apostle Paul wrote, *"Let the peace of Christ rule in your hearts"* (Colossians 3:15).

Peace, therefore, has a direct connection to godliness and to personal happiness. And peace is the attribute that God has provided to stand guard over our hearts in order to keep us from straying from his ways. But peace is derived from wisdom. True wisdom will create peace in a person's heart and life. It will lift the spirit. In fact, wisdom and peace are closely aligned. They have a common heritage in that the believer is encouraged to pursue them both. While Solomon tells us to pursue wisdom (see Proverbs 2:1-5), the Peter tells us to "seek peace and pursue it" (I Peter 3:11).

Third, the wisdom that comes from heaven is considerate. It is not forceful or harsh. The wisdom that leads to peace always taps gently on the door to one's heart and kindly asks for permission to enter. Only when wisdom has been rejected does it raise its voice to gain our attention. Typically, wisdom is meek, modest, and kind in all regards.

Fourth, true wisdom is submissive. In other words, it yields to others. It listens more frequently than it speaks. Wisdom takes seriously the observation that God has created man with two ears but only one mouth, because God wants people to listen twice as much as they talk.

Wisdom can only be obtained by noticing what others are doing and listening to what others are saying. By paying attention to others and to their words, a person can increase his knowledge and broaden his understanding. A person who is capable of yielding the floor and who is "quick to listen, slow to speak" (James 1:19) is a person who will make many wise decisions over the course of his life.

Fifth, the wisdom that comes from heaven is full of mercy and good fruits. Like God, a wise man or woman will show compassion toward others, as well as a willingness to forgive. The wise person will remember his own youthful failings and will be more inclined than most to offer mercy to those who are still navigating the treacherous pathway to maturity. The fruit of the Spirit includes patience, kindness, goodness, and gentleness. The man or woman who is wise will typically exhibit these qualities in their dealings with others.

Sixth, genuine wisdom is impartial. It is fair and unbiased, unprejudiced and evenhanded. A truly wise person will be swayed only by truth, not by coercion and certainly not by manipulation. God's principles will guide him, and he will never be held in contempt by those who hold a different view, because even they will realize that he is objective in all his dealings.

Finally, God's wisdom is sincere. It is never polluted with hypocrisy; it is always based on truth. It is never contaminated with deceit; it is always marked with honesty. It is never stained with pretense; it is always transparent and true. God's wisdom has nothing to hide in fact or in motivation. God's wisdom brings light and communicates life to all concerned.

To have this kind of wisdom is to have the heartbeat of God. To have this kind of understanding is to have the awareness of God. No matter what may come your way, you will always be equipped to handle it if your mind has been renewed and your soul has been saturated with wisdom. The wisdom of the Lord can lift your spirit and guide you through any challenge that life can send your way.

Dr. Myles Munroe says, "Wisdom is the ability to make use of knowledge effectively." So in a day and age when information is readily available, wisdom is sorely needed. Due to the increased availability of higher education and due to rapid advancements in technology and communication, people now have more data in their heads and at their fingertips than ever before. But few of them have understanding. Few of them have wisdom. So people perish for lack of knowledge. Even "my people" perish from the lack of properly applied information.

The mind is a powerful tool, and it can hold an incredible amount of data. But without wisdom, we are empty as human beings even though our heads are full. We are vessels wandering aimlessly in search of our potential and our destiny. We are lost without moorings. We are tossed by the ever-shifting winds of popular opinion and the ever-changing waves of circumstance. We have no foundation upon which to stand as we attempt to build our lives. We have no ground beneath our feet.

Wisdom, however, is a combination of discernment, judgment, and tact. It arms its possessor with the ability to distinguish between right and wrong, between good and bad, and between that which imparts "life" and that which imparts "death." It equips its owner with the ability to make right judgments with the facts at hand rather than judgments based on unfounded ideals or ungrounded fantasies. And it endows its owner with the ability to sense the time and the manner in which to employ its power. When God's mind is imparted to us through wisdom, we will always have great success in all that we do.

Most turmoil in life flows from folly, and folly flows from a lack of wisdom. To avoid folly, therefore, and to avoid the unrest that accompanies it, seek wisdom. Pursue wisdom. Like many of the wonderful gifts of God, this gift awaits those who value it and follow after it. Wisdom will not fall on us from above, and it will never sneak up on us while we sleep at night. The opening pages of Proverbs make it clear that wisdom is available only to those who value it highly and pursue it intentionally. Wisdom is acquired, not inherited. It is attained, not discovered.

But if you commit yourself to its pursuit and if you cherish it above life's temporal distractions, wisdom can become the most prized possession of your life, the only possession that can make the rest of life's pleasures more valuable and more rewarding. More than any other virtue, wisdom can bring success, happiness, peace, and confidence. Wisdom can lift your spirit.

MODULE 2

WHEN I KNOW, I GROW

WHEN I KNOW, I GROW

1. What is your primary occupation? Why is wisdom necessary in your line of work? How can wisdom bring success to you in your professional pursuits?

_____

_____

_____

2. God said, "My people are destroyed from lack of knowledge." How can godly people be destroyed simply because they lack understanding?

_____

_____

_____

3. God will protect us from our enemies, but he won't always protect us from ourselves. Can you give an example from your own life where God refused to protect you from yourself? What lesson did you learn from this experience?

_____

_____

_____

4. Have you ever asked God for wisdom? What specific situation caused you to make this request? Did God answer your prayer? How?

_____

_____

_____

5. As a person grows older, that person tends to place increasing value and increasing significance on the more fundamental elements of life, including wisdom. Is this true of you? Have you seen a noticeable change in your attitude toward knowledge and understanding as you grow older?

_____

_____

_____

6. Do you know someone personally that you would regard as an exceptionally wise person? Why do you view the person in this way? What makes this individual wise in your eyes?

_____

_____

_____

7. Do you know someone personally who seems to have an almost limitless reservoir of information in his or her head, yet who lacks the ability to utilize that information to make sound decisions? Does this person help you better understand the difference between possessing information and possessing wisdom?

_____

_____

_____

8. What does it mean to you personally when God talks about "renewing your mind"? Explain!

_____

_____

_____

9. Why do you think so many people embrace the belief that the course of their lives is determined by the stars, by the alignment of the planets, or by some other force of nature that is beyond their control?

_____

_____

_____

10. Wisdom will not fall on you from above, and it will never sneak up on you while you sleep at night and force its way into your life. In your opinion, how can a person acquire wisdom?

_____

_____

_____

DIGGING DEEPER

According to Christine Martin, wisdom can definitely impact the quality of your life and can definitely affect the state of your mind.

In your experience, how has the acquisition of knowledge and wisdom impacted the quality of your life?

_____

_____

_____

From your own personal perspective, how has the acquisition of knowledge and wisdom affected your state of mind?

_____

_____

_____

TWO PATHWAYS TO WISDOM

If any of you lacks wisdom, you should ask God,
who gives generously to all without finding fault,
and it will be given to you.
James 1:5

According to the Bible, there are two ways to obtain wisdom from the Lord: We can ask for his wisdom and we can seek his wisdom. The full context of Scripture, therefore, teaches us to do both.

God can and does impart wisdom to those who need it when they ask God for his wisdom. From time to time, all of us need a sudden infusion of wisdom. Faced with a big decision and little time to make it, a person must somehow find the resources to make the best and the most informed decision under the circumstances. In these and other similar situations, God will often impart wisdom to us through his Holy Spirit. He will speak to our minds and touch our hearts, leading us by providence or by the sense of peace that is imparted through his Holy Spirit.

But there's another kind of wisdom that God requires us to pursue (see Proverbs 4:7; Ecclesiastes 7:25). The foundational wisdom that undergirds our lives is a wisdom that must be built and accumulated over a lifetime by listening, reading, and following accomplished men and women and by experiencing the harsh realities of life for ourselves. This kind of wisdom must be purposely sought and pursued. It must be treasured and valued. It will not force itself upon anyone. Rather, it is reserved for the person who reveres wisdom and who truly desires it.

So ask God for wisdom. Ask the Lord to provide you with wisdom in those situations where you desperately need it. But also ask him to teach you to pursue it in your everyday life by learning from others and by learning from life itself. God will grant you the wisdom you desire.

SOMETHING TO THINK ABOUT

In the context of this study, we have seen that wisdom can "keep" a person, "rebuke" a person, "save" a person, and do other things to impact or change a person in multiple ways.

Solomon declares that wisdom has the ability to "save you" (Proverbs 2:12). How can wisdom "save" a person? Has wisdom "saved" you in any way?

_____

_____

_____

Solomon also taught that wisdom has the ability to "prolong your life" (Proverbs 3:2). How can wisdom prolong the life of the one who acquires it?

_____

_____

_____

Solomon said that wisdom has the capacity to "make your paths straight" (Proverbs 3:6). What does this mean to you, and how has wisdom made the paths of your life straight for you?

_____

_____

_____

MY PRAYER FOR WISDOM

Father, every day in every way, I face the challenges of living in an unjust world. I need your wisdom. I need to know what you know. I need to understand what you already understand. I need to be able to see myself, my situation, and my world through your eyes. I desperately need to know what you would do if you were standing here beside me. Jesus, when you were here among us, you always seemed to know exactly how to answer a question, exactly how to respond to a challenge, and exactly how to confront those who opposed you and the message you came to preach. Give me your heart, and give me your mind. Teach me your ways. Give me your understanding, your knowledge, and your wisdom. With it, I cannot fail. Without it, I cannot succeed. In Jesus' name, Amen!

MY SPIRITUAL JOURNAL

Take a few moments to record your thoughts regarding this week's session on knowing and growing in wisdom. What new things did you learn? What new insights and revelations have you had? What life-changing truths did Christine Martin impart that have impacted your thinking? What changes will you make in the days ahead?

_____

_____

_____

FOOD FOR THOUGHT

The Bible describes God's Words as spiritual bread and spiritual meat. It is designed to nourish the spirit and the soul in the same way that food nourishes the body. So read the following scripture every day this week, repeating it out loud when you read it, and memorize it, if possible. And while you meditate upon this passage, make notes about anything you may observe about your personal life and any changes you may want to make.

Blessed is the man who finds wisdom, the man who gains understanding, for she is more profitable than silver and yields better returns than gold. She is more precious than rubies; nothing you desire can compare with her. Long life is in her right hand; in her left hand are riches and honor. Her ways are pleasant ways, and all her paths are peace. She is a tree of life to those who embrace her; those who lay hold of her will be blessed.

Proverbs 3:13-18

_____

_____

_____

WISDOM FROM ABOVE

My people are destroyed from lack of knowledge.
Hosea 4:6

Be transformed by the renewing of your mind. Then you will be able to test and approve what God's will is—his good, pleasing and perfect will.
Romans 12:2

But the wisdom that comes from heaven is first of all pure; then peace-loving, considerate, submissive, full of mercy and good fruit, impartial and sincere.
James 3:17

COULD YOU REPEAT THAT?

You can never rise above the level of wisdom you have achieved.

Foolishness is obvious, but wisdom is discreet.

Wisdom is acquired, not inherited. It is attained, not discovered.

IN A NUTSHELL

Wisdom is the most important quality for success in life. With it, all other virtues can be acquired. Without it, no other virtues really matter.

CHAPTER 3

A Winning Attitude

When it comes to the all-important issue of attitude, there is no shortage of clichés floating around. You've heard them. I've heard them:

- Your attitude determines your altitude.
- You can't be a smart cookie with a crummy attitude.

You and I both know that these profundities ring true. At the same time, they seem rather hollow because they are so meaningless in practical terms and so unattainable. But they are unattainable because of the things that run through our minds when we think of "attitude." What is attitude? What does the word mean exactly?

The word attitude means "a bodily posture expressing mood; a mannerism displaying one's thoughts or feelings; one's disposition or opinion." According to the New Oxford American Dictionary, attitude is "a settled way of thinking or feeling about someone or something, typically one that is reflected in a person's behavior."

Attitude, therefore, is everything. It certainly affects everything. It guides our emotions; it directs our behaviors. It determines our actions; it governs our thoughts. Along with wisdom, it is undoubtedly one of the controlling factors of life. The attitude you hold today will definitely determine the outcome of your life tomorrow.

In fact, if you think about it, attitude is the primary thing that separates the believer from the unbeliever. The Bible tells us that God *"causes his sun to rise on the evil and the good, and sends rain on the righteous and the unrighteous"* (Matthew 5:45), so the natural processes of life have nothing to do with belief and unbelief. The Bible makes it clear that all men, regardless of their faith, will endure hardship (see John 16:33), so pain and suffering are not the distinguishing characteristics of belief and unbelief. And all men will be forced, at one time or another, to *"walk through the valley of the shadow of death"* (Psalm 23:4), so difficulty in life is not the pivotal distinction between the person of faith and the person without faith.

If I am reading my Bible correctly, there is one overriding distinction between the believer and the unbeliever, and that distinction is how each one chooses to view the sun that rises on his life every morning, how he chooses to walk through the valleys of life. The Christian man or woman doesn't have a choice whether to walk through life's valleys; God has destined all of us to face certain injustices and pains. But while the unbeliever walks through his valleys alone and without guidance or hope, the believer is supposed to walk through his valleys with the full assurance that God is with him and with the confidence that he will emerge triumphant on the other side. And this assurance and confidence, if genuine, are supposed to be evident in the way the believer behaves while he is in the midst of the valley. The believer is expected to exude certainty and hopeful expectation while he is traveling through the darkness.

The fact is that your attitude determines the outcome of your life, and the fact is that you have the power to control your attitude. You don't have to allow your attitude to control you. Especially if you are a Christian, you have the God-given ability to revolutionize your life and to soar to new heights of success and personal fulfillment. Whether your attitude is positive, negative, or somewhere in between, you have the ability to understand the forces that impact your attitude, and you have the ability to take control of those forces. You have the ability to take control of your own thought processes and to turn your mind over to God, unleashing all the potential that is being hindered by negative thinking and by a toxic disposition that is less than glorifying to the Lord.

Do you need an attitude adjustment? Do you need a change in the way you think or feel about life or in the way that you allow your thoughts and feelings to shape your moods and behaviors? Most of us do need a change, but most of us are blind to our own need for change. So we become defensive and start making excuses for ourselves when confronted with this critical question. But the fact remains that something is causing you to feel agitated. Something is causing you to feel frustrated. Something is causing you to feel bitter, incomplete, unfulfilled, or confrontational.

Just ask yourself a few simple questions and you will quickly see that your attitude is a lot more of a potent force in your life than you may have realized:

- Why am I having such a bad day?
- What causes my emotions to flare up so easily?
- What is the real "root" of the problem I am facing?
- Would Jesus act this way if he were in my situation?
- What does the Bible say about the way I should act under these circumstances?

You can't blame your feelings and behaviors on your problems, because everyone else is facing similar problems, yet many of these people are facing their problems with joy and assurance. You can't blame your feelings and behaviors on other people, because everyone else is dealing with the same annoying people who annoy you, yet many of them are dealing with these bothersome people in a constructive and redemptive way. And you can't blame your feelings and behaviors on your upbringing or your heritage or your temperament or your environment, because many others are demonstrating in the face of similar challenges that they can rise above these various influences and establish a new and more effective way of handling life's inevitable problems.

Sooner or later, you are going to have to face the fact that you are out of excuses. You are going to have to face the fact that your own thinking is shaping your destiny. You are going to have to confront the issue of your own attitude. As I have done, you are going to have to schedule an appointment with God for a divine intervention that will force you to take a long, hard look at your own thought processes and the lens through which you view your life. You are going to have to awaken to the reality that your perspective on life is shaping the direction of your life.

When some people look at their lives, they see only problems. When others look at a similar life path, they see abundant opportunities. While some see only obstacles and impediments on their daily schedules, others see wonderful experiences and the joy of interacting with others. While some see endless repetition and a meaningless existence, others see a chance to smell the roses and to enjoy the beauty of God's creation. Both groups are seeing the same sights and hearing the same sounds. But while one group concludes that life is a bother, the other concludes that life is a reward. And the only thing that distinguishes these two groups is their perspective, their attitude toward the lives they are living.

Running the risk that I might be construed as cold and insensitive, let me say that a person's attitude can be controlled if that person will learn to yield to the Holy Spirit. In fact, if you look at the full description of the Spirit-led life as it is defined by the apostle Paul in Galatians 5:22-23, the final, undergirding expression of Spirit-directed living is "self-control." And the self-controlled, Spirit-led life manifests itself in several obvious ways. It manifests itself through love, not hatred; through joy, not sadness; through peace, not internal strife; through patience, not impatience; through kindness, not cruelty; through goodness, not folly; through faithfulness, not unfaithfulness; through gentleness, not harshness. Yet most of us, if we were honest, would admit that we typically express ourselves in hateful, sorrowful, tumultuous, impatient, cruel, and belligerent ways when we have a bad attitude. So the constant tug of the Holy Spirit upon our hearts is designed to take us in a direction that is contrary to the path defined by a bad attitude.

But in the constant battle that is being waged between the person we are and the person we want to be, obvious questions arise, especially for the believer: Is it possible to change my attitude? Is it necessary? And if it is possible to modify my attitude, how can I create a new attitude?

Personally, I believe that an individual can change his or her perspective on life. If that weren't possible, the Christian faith would be ineffective and the Bible would be untrue. But since the Bible teaches us that it is possible to "put off the old man" and to "put on the new man" (see Colossians 3:9-10), I believe that a person, with some effort and a sincere desire to change, can definitely modify his or her outlook on life and on the everyday things of life that typically arouse that person's ire.

But this is where real faith is divided from superficial faith. Many people claim to be Christians, but real Christianity invites change. In fact, real Christianity requires change. If your faith doesn't change you, then your faith isn't true. But when something is true and we embrace it and accept it as true, that truth has the power to set us free (see John 8:32) and to change our lives from the inside out. Faith, if it is based upon something genuine, has the power to radically alter our lives. It has the power to impart life and to push back the forces of death and darkness that have crept into our lives.

The attitude you now exhibit is actually an acquired trait that can be "unlearned" and relearned the proper way. More than likely, your perspective on life was instilled in you by your family and your environment, and it has been reinforced by a lifetime of destructive thinking and behavior. It has been strengthened and confirmed by the words of your own mouth and with the encouragement of your friends. But now that you are a Christian, you have a choice. You don't have to accept the attitude the world handed to you and that your sinful nature has nurtured within you. You can renounce the attitude of "death" that you normally exhibit. You can repent of it, turn around, and, with the help and guidance of the Holy Spirit, create a whole new way of viewing the world.

If all you have known throughout your lifetime is negativity and defeat, then your mind may need to be reconditioned to see things in a whole new way. But that's okay. God specializes in renewing the mind of the believer. In fact, that is God's primary occupation in his church today. He is busy, not modifying the thinking of his people, not adjusting it, and not improving it or restoring it. He is busy "renewing" the mind of the person who would be his disciple (see Romans 12:2). He wants to completely tear down what the world and society have instilled in the minds of his children, and he wants to redeem the minds of those who have turned their lives over to him. He wants to completely renew their minds. And this means that God also wants to renew the believer's attitude: his attitude toward God, his attitude toward himself, and his attitude toward others and toward life itself.

I grew up in an environment that completely warped my thinking. For most of my life, my starting point for every experience was a negative one. My default position was one of defeat, blame, and victimization. According to my natural paradigm of life, the glass was always half empty, not half full. From my normal perspective, the day was always half over, not half remaining. And through the lens of my own outlook, everybody was out to get me, not out to benefit me or to enrich my life. The world was one big conspiracy theory, and I was its primary target.

But I finally had a rude awakening. I finally realized that this kind of thinking is poison to the soul. It is a state of darkness and despair that isn't even real. It is a form of methodical destruction that I impose upon myself by my own willful denial of the way God has taught me to think and my own willful acceptance of a mindset that is openly opposed to "whatever is true, whatever is noble, whatever is right, whatever is pure, whatever is lovely, whatever is admirable" (Philippians 4:8).

So I decided to change. I decided to do something about myself. And the more I thought about it, the more excited I became about the potential transformation of my thinking, because I soon came to realize that, once I had changed my thinking, everything else would fall into place. I realized that my thinking controls my attitude and my attitude controls my destiny. So I knew that to allow God to do spiritual surgery on my mind was to allow him to correct everything in my life that needed his divine touch.

Has the process been easy? No, it hasn't. I'm not going to lie to you. But it has been fruitful, and it has been extremely rewarding. Like a diet, an exercise program, or any other new discipline, the effort to renew my mind has been a battle against human nature. The journey has been rife with temptations, and the pathway of progress has been marred with ups and downs. So my progress has been incremental, not steady or rapid. But, over time, I have seen progress, real progress. And I know that as long as I continue to feed my mind with positive thoughts every day, I am going to continue to break the power of my bad habits of negative thinking, and I am going to develop a new way of approaching life. In fact, I already have done this to a great extent.

But let me go back to the analogy of a diet or an exercise program. There is a cold, hard reality of life that we typically confront whenever we engage any new effort to improve our health, whether that effort involves physical health, emotional health, or spiritual health. The tendency of human nature is to do nothing and hope that our health will improve on its own. But health never improves by ignoring obvious problems and hoping they will just get better. Rather, improving one's health is like pushing a boulder uphill. It is hard, tedious work that progresses an inch at a time. And if you take a break for just one minute, the boulder can roll back down the hill and you can lose all the progress you worked so hard to achieve. But if you can manage to push that boulder forward just one or two inches a day and not relent, you will eventually get the boulder to the top of the hill and you can look out over your domain from a new perspective high above the rest of the world. People will notice the change, and they will reward you accordingly. You will notice the change too, and God will reward you accordingly.

Like any element of your health, attitude is a little thing that makes a big difference. And like any element of your health, you have the power to do something about your attitude. You can change it. You can make it better. And God is here to help.

In fact, if you were to ask me to define the Christian life, I would tell you that the Christian life is the cradle-to-grave process of allowing God to bridge the gap between those things we believe and those things we actually experience for ourselves in life. Thank God for his mercy and his grace. We are forgiven and accepted upfront, before we get things right. But once we surrender our lives to the Lord and ask him to save us from our sins, he takes that prayer very seriously, and he sends his Holy Spirit into our hearts to start the lifelong process of renewing our minds and transforming our attitudes so that our behaviors eventually catch up with our beliefs. Sooner or later, he is going to get us to the top of the hill. Sooner or later, he is going to enable us to bring our lives in alignment with the things we believe and profess.

So quit beating yourself up because your attitude isn't what it should be right now. Quit punishing yourself for the way you are. Realize that you are the product of many years of negative programming. You are the product of many years of worldly brainwashing. You didn't develop your current mindset overnight, so you won't develop a new perspective on life overnight. But you must begin the long, arduous process of adjusting the way you think. You must allow God to rewire your brain and do spiritual surgery on your mind. You must let the Holy Spirit help you create a new way of looking at the world. And you must believe that you have what it takes to make this necessary journey and that God will be there every step of the way to forgive you and help you. He has already forgiven you. But now he wants to actually change you.

So hold on, and don't give up. Don't be impatient either. But as you prepare to begin this rewarding journey, let me offer you some good advice from God's Word that can help you make the transition.

First, shed some tears along the way.

Why are so many people afraid to cry? Why are so many people afraid to show intense emotions? God made us to be emotional creatures. In fact, emotions make life worth living. To "feel" something is to truly experience it.

Now obviously, there is an appropriate time and an appropriate place to express one's emotions. It is unfair to others to dump your emotions on them when they least expect it and when they really don't want to deal with them. In fact, if you think about it, that's really what a bad attitude is all about: dumping our emotions verbally and through excessive body language on someone who doesn't want to deal with those emotions and at a time he isn't expecting their arrival.

But I believe all of us could be psychologically and spiritually healthier if we could just learn to release our emotions in proper ways. For instance, I notice that many people shed tears when they worship the Lord in church, and I think this is wonderful. If genuine worship can't touch your soul, nothing can. As long as your tears aren't out of place and as long as your emotions don't distract others from worshiping God, I believe that worship is a very appropriate time to release your deepest emotions to the Lord. In fact, I don't often analyze people during worship, because I am busy worshiping the Lord myself. But when I do open my eyes and glance around at those people who are touching heaven, I see some people weeping, some people smiling, and some people laughing. I think it's great.

People in the Bible seemed to be intensely emotional. They didn't just cry; they wailed. They didn't just rejoice; they danced. They didn't just repent; they shaved their heads, put on sackcloth, and sat in a pile of ashes for several days or weeks. When they mourned, everyone knew they were mourning. And when they celebrated, they did so with flutes and tambourines. They knew how to release their deepest sorrows and grief, but they also knew how to celebrate with merriment whenever they received good news.

Occasionally, there are places in the Bible where God challenged people for their displays of emotion ("Why are you angry? Why is your face downcast?" in Genesis 4:6). But most of the time, God simply took note of people's feelings. And at times, he, too, was emotionally moved. God "laughs" (Psalm 2:4) and "Jesus wept" (John 11:35). In addition, the Lord is portrayed in the Scriptures as experiencing joy, sorrow, jealousy, and a whole range of emotions that are normally linked to humanity.

The key here for the believer is to know the right time and the right place to express his emotions and the right way to display them. My husband is not my punching bag. My son is not my anger management therapist. Even when my emotions are raging, I should always remember that my words have the power of life and death, and it is impossible to take them back later. So I must learn to release my emotions, but I must learn to release them in the right way and to the right people.

The Bible tells us that there is "a time to weep and a time to laugh, a time to mourn and a time to dance" (Ecclesiastes 3:4). So there is nothing sinful in any legitimate emotion. There is nothing evil in the expression of any authentic feeling, even anger (see Ephesians 4:26). But the key to managing one's emotions is to know the proper time to release an emotion and the proper way to express it.

It is always appropriate to show one's honest emotions to the Lord. That's why I recommend that you use your daily prayer time to express some of your deepest feelings to God. In fact, if you don't give your emotions to the Lord during your daily prayer time, you're probably going to dump those emotions on some innocent, unsuspecting soul later that day. So you might as well deal with your feelings at the start of the day or before going to bed at night rather than carrying them around with you until they fester into a poisonous sore.

When something bad happens, when a relationship is threatened, when somebody hurts you unfairly, when a loved one dies, your emotions are affected. There's nothing wrong with that. God designed you to feel the feelings that you feel. Grief and even anger are legitimate responses to many of life's events, and that is why God keeps a record of every tear we shed and why he will spend some significant time dealing with all those tears as soon as we get to heaven (see Revelation 21:4).

There is a natural grieving process through which the human soul passes whenever that soul has been deprived, threatened, or wounded. And the length and depth of that process is different for every person. I don't know why some people seem to recover more quickly than others when life hands them a lemon, and I don't know why some people respond better to life's challenges and disappointments. But these two things I do know: I do know that the suffering will pass, and I do know that God has given every person the ability to discharge the deadly poison that accumulates within the soul as a result of these spiritual wounds by releasing that poison through one's emotions.

At the same time, however, God expects us to control our emotions, not to be controlled by our emotions. It's a little like sneezing. You can't control the urge to sneeze. Sneezing is God's way of clearing the air passages. But you do get to choose which way to turn your head and whether to cover your mouth. If you sneezed on me, I would be appropriately angry, because I know that you have the power to control that urge.

So it is never appropriate for me to throw a pity party. Ungodly displays of emotion are selfish and manipulative. They are immature. Know where to draw the line with your emotions, and know how to limit and control their expression. At the same time, however, learn to let it all out: your fears, your sorrows, and your regrets. Get in touch with your true feelings whenever anything is bothering you, and deal with those feelings now, before they become toxic. Go to God in prayer. Get in his presence and let him draw all that emotional venom out of you. Then create a better memory and a happier attitude. And instead of letting your unbridled display of negative emotions sour everyone around you, let the more positive emotions of your friends and family members lift you up. Remember, your attitude determines your altitude.

Second, learn to appreciate the gift of laughter.

On September 11, 2001, the United States was attacked in a vicious and cruel way that will endure forever in the memories of the American people. In fact, the crimes committed that day were so heinous and so demonic that nobody was prepared for them. No pool of thinkers had ever even imagined the possibility of such an act.

If you are old enough to remember the events of that day and the days immediately following, you will recall the deep sense of grief that impacted our nation. You will also remember how that grief led to a sudden and dramatic change in the way we conducted our daily lives. Flights were canceled, weddings were delayed, and even professional football games were postponed, because nobody felt like participating in the normal celebrations of life. But on September 29, less than three weeks after the terrorist attacks on New York and Washington, Saturday Night Live, one of America's iconic television programs, launched its twenty-seventh season of network broadcasting.

At first, the producers of Saturday Night Live were apprehensive about returning to the airwaves. They were concerned about injecting humor into the national consciousness too soon. Was it inappropriate? Was it arrogant? But when New York City Mayor Rudy Giuliani offered to appear on the show along with many of New York's finest firemen and police officers, plans moved forward to intrude upon the national spirit of mourning with a flagrant display of unabashed comedy. And the nation responded warmly. In fact, like a person starving for nourishment, the people of this country embraced the humor and welcomed the laughter.

The Bible tells us that laughter is an essential thing and a very positive force in life. Ecclesiastes 3:4, which we quoted earlier, reminds us that there is "a time to weep and a time to laugh." So, according to God, laughter, when enjoyed at the proper time, is a good thing. In fact, God says it is a necessary thing and likens it to medication for the soul. King Solomon, the wisest man who ever lived, writes, *"A joyful heart is good medicine."* (Proverbs 17:22, NASB). *And Bildad, who was try-*

*ing to walk his good friend, Job, through the worst days of his
personal suffering, said, "(God) will yet fill your mouth with
laughter and your lips with shouts of joy"* (Job 8:21).

Nothing can lift your spirit quite like a good, old-fashioned belly roll. When I'm feeling down, nothing picks me
up like getting together with someone who can make me forget my cares long enough to get downright silly. I don't recommend this as a way of life, but, when you're feeling blue,
your whole world can change if you can just get with that one
person who can make you crack up and laugh so hard that
you can't breathe and your side starts splitting with pain.

I'm fortunate to have a couple of people like that in my
life. My sister makes me laugh a lot. In fact, when I'm strug-
gling emotionally, I pick up the phone and call her. I'm sure
that we sound like a couple of giddy schoolgirls when we are
talking to one another. But when I need to laugh, I don't really care. And my husband could have been a professional
comedian. He is always in a positive mood, and he still has
the ability to make me laugh at will. You, too, need to get
away from depressing people and spend more time with people who can make you laugh. And if you don't have enough
people like that in your life, then watch a funny movie, read
a funny book, or check out the comics in your daily newspaper. But learn to laugh again. It's healthy for you.

Once again, let me take you back to your childhood.
There's a reason that Jesus told us to become like little chil-

dren. There are some things we had figured out when we were kids, but somewhere along the line we forgot those fundamental lessons of life, and we have suffered as a result of that loss. One of the things we have forgotten as adults is how to play. When we were children, we knew how to laugh and play. We knew how to get away from all our problems for just a little while by getting together with other children and quickly morphing into the make-believe world of fantasy and laughter. But when we became adults, we started taking ourselves far too seriously, and we forgot how to do these natural, childlike things.

Just think about it! When you were seven years old, you could have had the worst day imaginable at school. But once you got home, you forgot all about it. How? You went outdoors to meet up with your little friends, and all of you started playing and laughing. You started slipping into an imaginary world of princesses and soldiers, secret agents and mermaids. You forgot about everything around you. You even lost track of the time. And by the time you were thrust back into reality by your mother's call to dinner, your emotional engines were recharged and your emotional strength was restored. The tiny respite from grief that your short time of laughter afforded you was a respite that gave you the resolve you needed for the battle ahead.

Children play; even animals play. But adults have forgotten how to laugh, especially a lot of Christian adults. In fact, some of the sourest people I know are Christian people who haven't smiled in so many years, I'm afraid their faces might crack and bleed if they suddenly tried to fake a smile. I don't know why so many believers equate spirituality with somberness. Obviously, we want to take the Lord seriously. But there's no reason to take ourselves so seriously. Besides, we do ourselves more harm than good and we serve as pathetic and impotent witnesses when we live our lives with absolutely no sense of humor and remove from life all the joy that makes life worth living.

If you can learn to laugh at the things that are funny, you will eventually learn to laugh in the face of things that hurt. And if you can learn to not take yourself so seriously all the time, you can learn to grin and bear many of the ironies of life. A man who can roll with laughter is a man who can roll with the punches. So laugh a little, and grow a lot. A joyful and playful heart can lift your spirit.

Third, spend your time around positive people.

Forrest Gump's little girlfriend, Jenny Curran, used to say, "Run, Forrest, run!" Under the right circumstances, that's always good advice. And never was Jenny's advice more applicable than when it comes to the company we keep. If you tend to spend most of your time with negative people, then run as fast as you can. Get away from those people before you dry up like a dead leaf and completely turn to dust.

I do hope you are smart enough to know that nobody influences you more than your friends. Nothing shapes your attitudes and your behaviors more than the people with whom you associate. Attitudes are like the flu: You "catch" attitudes from other people. So if you spend most of your time around negative people, you are going to eventually develop a negative attitude. In fact, if you don't take on the negative attitude of your friends, you won't be in their group very long. Those people will force you into exile faster than you can say "woe is me" in order to preserve the prevailing attitude of doom and gloom that dominates their get-togethers.

The opposite is true, as well: If you spend most of your time around happy and positive people who tend to look on the bright side of things, you will soon start thinking and talking just like them. There is nothing that a group of high achievers hates more than a "victim" who wants to blame everybody and everything for the circumstances of his life. So accomplished people won't keep you around very long either if you don't share their zest for living.

If you want to be a winner, therefore, spend most of your time with winners. If you want to be successful, spend most of your spare time with successful people. And if you want to be happy, spend most of your time with happy people. Of course, you can't control everyone in your life. You don't always have a choice when it comes to your coworkers or your neighbors, and you can't even pick the other members of your own family. But you can control yourself, and you can choose your friends. So I strongly encourage you to spend as much time as possible with people that you want to emulate. If you want a good attitude, spend your time with those people who exhibit a good attitude. Spend time with those people who make you laugh and who help you see beyond your temporal problems to a way of life that can endure forever. Run away from people who pull you down, and run toward people who lift you up. This will elevate your spirit.

Fourth, become future oriented.

In 1998, when President Bill Clinton was being impeached by the United States House of Representatives, a political movement began, called Move On. In fact, when the impeachment failed in the United States Senate, the movement continued to grow and is now known as moveon.org. Even though I don't identify myself with the political positions of this organization, I do identify with their slogan. Somebody there had a great idea, because I like the sound of "moving on." There just comes a time in life when you need to put the past behind you and "move on" to better and brighter things.

When it comes to life and to the attitudes that drive life, I have noticed that there are basically two kinds of people: There are those who "move on," and there are those who cling to the past. Those who cling to the past tend to be miserable people. They tend to wallow in self-pity, and they tend to hold grudges and constantly pick at the scabs of their past emotional wounds. But those who "move on" to the future tend to be happier. They tend to release the disappointments and the heartaches of the past, and they tend to forget the pains of today as they busy themselves with the pursuit of tomorrow's rewards.

Some people just won't let go of yesterday. They hang onto their misery the same way they hang on to photographs of old boyfriends or to worn-out pairs of shoes. But with some effort, you can learn to let go of the things from your past that are holding you back, and you can learn to become one of those future-oriented people who can't wait to get up each morning so they can push their lives forward toward meaningful goals that motivate them.

It would help you in this transition if you could come to understand that nobody goes through life without having some bad experiences and without accumulating a few wounds. Nobody can fight the battles of life without picking up a few scars along the way. But whether you hold onto those bad experiences or use them as springboards to better things is a matter of personal choice. The Bible encourages you to *"put off… the old man"* and to *"put on the new man"* as *you are "renewed in the spirit of your mind"* (Ephesians 4:22-24, KJV), an obvious analogy that is intended to demonstrate the vastly superior path of making changes in the way you think. But the clear message here is that you must deliberately "put off" your old way of thinking before you can "put on" a new way of thinking.

You know what it's like to change clothes. In fact, you've done it so many times during your life, you don't even think about it while you are doing it. While you are mentally occupied with other things, you slip out of your work clothes and you slip into your jeans and t-shirt. But there's a certain order in which you perform this task, even when you aren't consciously thinking about your actions. First, you "put off" the clothes you are currently wearing; then you "put on" the comfortable outfit that you want to wear around the house. You can't put on something new until you take off something old. This is the message Paul is trying to convey to us about life and particularly about the process a person must engage if that person intends to renew the prevailing attitude of his mind.

Another way of thinking about this is to think of "stepping out" and "stepping in." You can't "step in" to a new job or a new apartment until you "step out" of the old one. Making any significant change in your life is always a two-step process. You have to "put off" the old and then "put on" the new. You have to "step out" of the old and then "step in" to the new.

The primary reason that people have difficulty moving on with their lives is because they are trapped in the past. The primary reason that people have difficulty "putting on" their new dreams and goals is because they haven't yet "put off" the heartbreaks of yesterday. The primary reason that people have a hard time "stepping in" to better relationships and better lives is because they cannot seem to "step out" of the old relationships, old behaviors, and old thinking that is restricting their forward motion and hindering them in the pursuit of excellence.

Life is not fair, but we have a God who is fair. If something in your past is negatively affecting your life today and negatively impacting the way you want your life to be tomorrow, turn that thing over to the Lord and experience the power that comes with his love and the freedom that he imparts. If, with God's help, you can find a way to move on with your life and set your eyes upon future ambitions rather than past disappointments, you can be happy again. You can be so consumed with the future that you practically forget the past.

So refuse to dwell on the bad times of the past, and they will lose their power over you. Happiness is never found in the past; happiness is always found in the present and the future.

Fifth, develop a healthy self-image.

To maintain a positive attitude, you must develop a good self-image. This is especially true in a highly competitive and confrontational world.

The world in which we live is a world marked with conflict. I have thought about this for a long, long time, and I have concluded that most of life's pains arise from life's conflicts and most of life's conflicts arise, not from evil, but from the competitive and confrontational nature of life. Just think about this for a moment.

How many run-ins did you have today with friends, salesmen, coworkers, or family members? Nobody got up this morning with the intention of making your life more difficult. But as you went about your daily routines and your personal responsibilities, your tasks took you across the path of one of your friends, who was also going about her daily routines and responsibilities. And the two of you collided. Her goals came into conflict with your goals, and the two of you had an unpleasant encounter. That's not evil; that's just the nature of life in this cursed world. In fact, you can see this tendency toward conflict in nature itself. Even the two male birds sitting on the telephone wire in your backyard fight every afternoon over the top spot on the pole, and they fight every afternoon over the female bird that has recently joined them for their afternoon sing-along.

Life necessitates competition, and competition necessitates conflict. In fact, the Bible makes it clear that conflict is unavoidable in this world. But the Bible also makes it clear that the believer should engage these unavoidable conflicts with Christian grace and with patience, love, and forbearance. For the believer, it's not whether we will have conflict in this world; it's how we will navigate the conflicts of life.

With that said, I believe there are two primary qualities that the believer must possess in order to engage life's conflicts without being adversely affected by them. First, the believer must have a high regard for others and must learn how to love, defer, and forgive. Second, the believer must have a high regard for himself and must learn to appreciate his own value in the eyes of God. If not, he will be repeatedly trampled underfoot and will eventually develop a sickly self-image that leads to a bad attitude toward other people and toward life in general.

Don't get me wrong. Some of life's confrontations are not so innocent and pure. Some of them are driven by sin and are motivated by Hell itself. Sometimes, Satan has his hands all over the confrontations of life. As believers, we must learn to recognize these kinds of unnatural conflicts, and we must deal with them in strength and boldness while maintaining our spiritual integrity. But the vast majority of life's conflicts are not satanically inspired, nor do they result from sin. They are merely the natural consequence of two people with two opposing wills and two conflicting agendas crossing paths with one another and stepping on each other's toes in pursuit of their conflicting goals. In these kinds of conflicts, the believer must have a different kind of internal strength that can sustain him and help him stand his ground in the conflict (unless he purposely chooses to yield his ground through love, not manipulation, for the sake of the relationship or the benefit of the other person).

But your self-image is the all-determining factor in your

willingness and ability to fight for yourself in the midst of life's battles (or defer on purpose). Your body and mind are a thought factory, and you know when you feel worthy of prevailing in a fight. The stronger your feelings of adequacy and worthiness, the more likely you will be to prevail in the fight and the better you will feel about yourself as you lock horns with other determined people. But the weaker your feelings of adequacy and worthiness, the more likely you will be to surrender to the strong will of others and the less valuable and worthy of victory you will become in your own eyes. Then, over time, this can easily become a real problem as you actually start to despise yourself. An abnormally deflated ego will forever shape the way you view yourself and the way you relate to other people, whom you will typically avoid at all costs if you regard yourself as beneath them in some way.

Pride is the basis of all sin, and it was apparently the original sin of Satan himself (see Isaiah 14:12-17). But there are two kinds of pride: the sinful kind and the good kind. The sinful kind of pride causes a person to see himself in inflated terms. Under the influence of sinful pride, a person elevates himself above reality in his own mind. He convinces himself that he is stronger, smarter, faster, and morally superior to other people, and he starts looking down on others as a result of his inflated appraisal of his own worth. But the good kind of pride is the kind that causes a person to defend the dignity of his family name, to encourage his children to do their best in school, and to get choked up when he hears the Star Spangled Banner.

We Christians sometimes have a false sense of humility. We put ourselves down too easily and too quickly. In fact, there was a popular Christian song a number of years ago that said: "I'm nothing. I'm nobody. I'm no one. But someone made something of me." I have always appreciated the underlying sentiment of this song, but I disagree with the route the songwriter takes to make his point about God's grace.

The Bible never tells us to think of ourselves lowly. In fact, there are many instances in the Bible where God actually had to instruct people to stop thinking of themselves in such low terms and to start seeing their own value and potential. When God appeared to Moses at the burning bush and appointed him to confront Pharaoh on God's behalf, Moses complained that he lacked the talent to lead the Jewish people (see Exodus 10-11). Nevertheless, God saw Moses' potential for becoming the greatest leader in the history of Israel. When God appeared to Gideon while he was threshing wheat in a winepress and summoned Gideon to deliver the people of Israel from the oppressive hand of the Midianites, Gideon complained that he lacked the ability to do what God wanted him to do (see Judges 6:14-15). Nevertheless, God saw Gideon's potential to prevail in one of the most amazing military victories in history. And Saul, the first king of Israel, complained to the prophet Samuel that he was unworthy of becoming Israel's first king because he was "from the smallest tribe of Israel" and "the least of all the clans of the tribe of Benjamin"(I Samuel 9:21). Nevertheless, God instructed his prophet to anoint Saul as the first king of the Jewish people.

Paul, too, had his own struggles with self-image and self-worth. Because of his past history of persecuting the church and because of his direct involvement in the stoning of Stephen, Paul was scorned by many within the church and his apostleship was questioned throughout his lifetime. This caused Paul to see himself as "the least of the apostles" and a man who was unworthy of his title (see I Corinthians 15:9). Perhaps this is why God chose Paul as the recipient of one of the greatest biblical revelations regarding the difference between healthy pride and sinful pride when Paul wrote, *"Do not think of yourself more highly than you ought, but rather think of yourself with sober judgment"* (Romans 12:3).

But notice that this verse stops short of instructing believers to think of themselves lowly. This verse does not tell the believer to loathe himself, and it does not tell Christians to belittle themselves, to be ashamed of their abilities, or to hide under the bed and let others take the trophy or win the election. This verse simply tells the believer not to think of himself more highly than he ought. It tells the believer to evaluate himself honestly and with sober judgment.

In other words, Christian people should think highly of themselves. After all, we are children of God. We are offspring of the King. But there is a level above which our self-analysis becomes distorted, so we should never allow our self-estimation to rise above this level of reality. If we do, our egos will inflate and our heads will explode with unrighteous conceit and egotism. And this will lead to many additional forms of sin.

So learn to think highly of yourself, but don't think more highly of yourself than you ought. And be proud of what God has helped you achieve in your life, but don't be so proud that you fail to remember with gratitude God's ever-present help in your journey through life. When you recognize and embrace your own self-worth and your own potential, not only will you feel better about yourself, but you also will feel capable of confronting those things in your life that you desperately want to change and you will feel capable of confronting the difficult people in your life who trample on you and who undeservedly take the prize.

The better you feel about yourself, the harder it is to be oppressed. The more you nurture a positive outlook toward life and toward yourself, the more you will experience moments of victory in your life, which will create additional self-esteem, which will create additional victories. And the more that you succeed in life, the less likely you will be to slip back into the role of "victim."

The devil is a very smart adversary. He knows how to hit you where it hurts. He knows how to wait until you are down in the dumps to do his dirty work, because he is much more likely to manipulate you into a state of submission when you feel less capable of waging warfare against him. Nevertheless, thousands of years of observation have helped God's people learn the tactics of our enemy, and his tactics are ineffective when we have a healthy attitude toward ourselves. The man who sees value in himself is the man who will never surrender to the enemy. The woman who sees her own worth is the woman who will rise above any challenge. So learn to have a healthy self-image. The world can never defeat you when you have an honest appraisal of your own value and your own worth to God and others.

Sixth, seek shelter in God's presence.

The human body is designed for work. In fact, without work, we suffer physically and our bodies deteriorate. It is a good thing to work with your hands, to raise your heartbeat, and to perspire. But all of us know that we have limits to our physical abilities. I can lift a 20-pound bag of potatoes, and I can easily push a 15-pound vacuum cleaner around the house. But I cannot lift a 300-pound bag of cement, nor can I lift my car with one hand while I clean the grease spots beneath the car with the other hand.

But in the same way that God created me with physical limitations, he also created me with emotional limitations. The body of man and the soul of man both have their constraints. So why is it that I can understand the value of physical rest and its necessity to my overall health, yet I have difficulty comprehending the concept of spiritual and emotional rest?

If I have pushed myself hard for several days in a physical sense, I know that a couple of days of rest and relaxation can do me a world of good. But if I have pushed myself hard in an emotional sense, it often never occurs to me to seek a place of restoration for my soul. Nevertheless, Jesus said, *"Come unto me, all ye that labour and are heavy laden, and I will give you rest"* (Matthew 11:28, KJV).

One of the most effective things you can do to lift your spirit is to spend some time with the Lord. Are you carrying too much weight and too many responsibilities? Are your emotional shoulders weighed down with too many burdens and too many cares? Over time, all these pressures can destroy you from within and can absolutely devastate your attitude and even your zest for living.

I'm guilty of making this mistake in my own life. How about you? It's easy to let the pressures of work, the challenges of marriage, and the conflicts of life take their toll on us and leave us with crummy attitudes. It's easy to let the burdens and responsibilities of life pile up until our spirits sag beneath the weight. That's why it is so important for the child of God to spend some time with the Lord so that he can do for us in the spiritual arena what a good vacation can do in the physical arena.

God did not create you to carry the weight of the world on your back, but he did create you to enjoy fellowship with him. So if you are piling more and more weight on yourself, but you are avoiding intimacy with the Lord, you are burning the spiritual candle at both ends, and you are bound to crash sooner or later. But God can give you rest. He can take some of the weight off you. He can restore your soul (see Psalm 23:3). He can help you "mount up with wings as eagles" (Isaiah 40:31) and soar above it all. He can reinstate you and reinstate the good attitude toward life that was part of your personality before you bit off more than you could chew alone.

We were made for God. We were not made to live apart from God. So when we draw near to the Lord, something happens to us in a positive way. You know that feeling. You get it whenever you go to church. You can't quite explain it, but you leave church feeling better than you did when you arrived. It just makes us feel better to worship the Lord and to spend a few minutes in his presence.

But even though church is wonderful and even though there is significant value in worshiping with other believers, there is equal value in spending quality time alone with the Lord. And different people make use of this private time in different ways. Some people get rejuvenated whenever they spend time with the Lord. Other people cry when they enter God's presence, the type of crying that is cleansing and healing as they focus on God's presence and his glory. Others laugh in the presence of the Lord, and still others begin to see a pathway through the maze of life as God gives them hope or helps them refocus their priorities.

Time with the Lord is healing. Time with the Lord is restorative. Time with the Lord is cathartic, therapeutic, and inspiring. Time with the Lord is a time of renewal and edification (the improvement of oneself morally or intellectually). A half hour spent in the Lord's presence at the beginning of each day can totally reshape the remainder of that day and can place the events of that day on a higher plane. It can equip the believer with the necessary resources for bearing the day's burdens and fighting the day's battles.

When we learn to enter God's presence and to lay our burdens at his feet while we talk to him and listen to him, we emerge from that encounter with a sense that the load has been lightened. Consequently, we tend to act more like God. We tend to see the world through his eyes, recognizing everything that happens around us as either a challenge or an opportunity that needs to be confronted accordingly. We tend to speak more positively and to love more practically throughout the day, with patience, forbearance, and grace. We tend to be more successful in what we do, because we approach our responsibilities with an attitude that demonstrates strength, resolve, and expectation that flow from an accurate sense of personal value and worth.

But when we carry our burdens all day without the assistance of God, we begin to live in turmoil, and our lives become saturated with ever-increasing stress. Eventually, the chaotic nature of life overtakes us, and we change, not for the better, but for the worse. Slowly, we begin to lose our love for ourselves and others. We begin to feel threatened and intimidated, so we demonstrate rising hostility. We start making mistakes we might otherwise avoid, and we start having deeper and increasingly costly conflicts with those who should be our allies in the challenges of life. So guilt and frustration fill our lives, and a deepening sense of loss takes over.

Listen! You are not Superman or Wonder Woman. You are not designed to handle life alone, especially in this modern age when the pressures of life are multiplied and the pace of life is accelerated. The more you take upon yourself in pursuit of your dreams and your destiny, the more you need to spend time with the Lord. The more you bite off the apple, the more help you need maintaining the roles you have assumed. Spending time with the Lord can definitely lift your spirit.

Attitude is the primary motivation behind everything we do. It is certainly a key factor in one's personal success and achievement and in one's satisfaction with life. Realizing that a person's attitude affects every other element of his life, I have attended countless seminars to learn how to master my own attitude. I have read hundreds of books and articles, and I have listened to hours upon hours of recorded messages on the subject. Over and over again, I have been reminded that nothing is more important than maintaining a positive attitude. In fact, I am now convinced that, outside of a personal relationship with God, the most valuable asset a person can possess is a positive attitude toward life.

Your attitude is usually one of the first things that people notice about you. You may not be able to change your height or your body type, but you can certainly change your attitude. And even though a good physical appearance has its upside, nothing can make you more attractive than a positive attitude and nothing can distract people from your otherwise attractive appearance more than a negative attitude. The Bible tells us that *"like a gold ring in a pig's snout is a beautiful woman who shows no discretion"* (Proverbs 11:22). So nothing is more important than your outlook on life. The judgment that you derive from your personal perspective determines the course of your life and determines other people's response to you.

An individual's attitude may be partially rooted in his or her genetics or environment, but attitude is more directly related to a person's self-esteem. Attitude is an acquired attribute that a person constructs within his own heart and mind over a lifetime, so it can be modified over time with proper nourishment and training. Your emotional health is rooted irrevocably in the way you view yourself, and your own self-perspective is rooted ultimately in your relationship with Jesus Christ. So if you have no relationship with Christ, it can be virtually impossible to develop a strong and healthy self-image. But if you do have a fulfilling relationship with the Lord, you should be in the process of creating a well-balanced view of yourself, a view that points to your utter dependency on the Lord, yet your infinite value to him as his special creation. After all, he died for you because of the value he placed upon your soul.

For the Christian, therefore, self-esteem must flow from Jesus Christ and from a proper understanding of the value God has placed upon the life of each individual. We are worthy because God has declared us to be worthy. We are valuable because God has determined that we are valuable. In fact, God has declared us to be more worthy and more valuable than we might imagine and certainly more valuable than we feel. Thus, reshaping our own view of ourselves to more accurately reflect the view that God has of us can truly revolutionize our lives. It can revitalize our thinking and "transform" our minds. It can give us a new attitude toward life and can lift our spirits.

The person with a good self-image that flows from a right understanding of his infinite value to God and his utter dependence on God is a person who will ultimately develop a healthy and positive attitude toward life. Spending time every day in prayer, this person will emerge from his prayer closet with positive words on his lips and with a realistic expectation of life. He will accept both the good and the incomplete elements in himself. He will appreciate and celebrate the differences that exist between him and others. He will be open to a relationship with God and with those who earn his respect and trust. And he will be able to express love freely and willingly, but always within the constraints of God's will.

Having confidence in God's love and in God's grace, the person with a healthy self-image will be able to recognize God's hand upon his life. He will be able to see the changes the Lord has made within him and the impact that God has made on others through him. Thus, his heart will be filled with gratitude and praise, and he will develop an ever-increasing appreciation for the power of God in his own life. Accordingly, he will be able to make use of his past failures. He will learn from them and move forward with a clear conscience and no regrets.

The person with a positive self-image can clearly see that God is able to more than compensate for anything that may be lacking in his life. And he will be able to see that the future growth and development made possible by God is a greater prize than the sorrows of past mistakes. So get ready to see a significant difference in how you view things. When you start making changes—tiny, incremental changes in your thinking and your perspective—your self-image will gradually improve and your life will gradually progress. You will learn to see the world and your future differently when you finally come to appreciate the fact that you were created in the likeness of God and when you finally become happy with the "you" that God created. A new perspective on life will definitely lift your spirit.

MODULE 3

A WINNING ATTITUDE

A WINNING ATTITUDE

1. The unbeliever typically walks through the valleys of life without guidance or hope while the believer has the opportunity to walk through the valleys of life with the full assurance that God is with him and with the confidence that he will emerge victorious on the other side. How do you typically walk through the dark valleys of life? Do you act more like a believer or an unbeliever? Why?

_____

_____

_____

_____

_____

2. Do you need a change in your attitude? What kind of change? Describe the specific things about your attitude that are not pleasing to you or to God.

_____

_____

_____

3. Do you believe it is possible to change your attitude? Do you think it is necessary to change? What is the first step you believe you should take in order to create a new way of viewing life?

_____

_____

_____

4. Christine Martin explains that, for many years, her default perspective on life was a perspective of defeat, blame, and victimization. Then her eyes were opened to see herself objectively, and she began the long process of changing the way she viewed her life. What is your "default" position on life? What is your typical way of viewing the events of life? What would you like your new default position to be?

_____

_____

_____

5. When it comes to the honest expression of emotions, the key for the believer is to know the right time and the right place to express emotions and the right way to display them.

Your spouse is not your punching bag. Your children are not your anger management therapists. Do you express emotions inappropriately? How? Do you express them to the wrong people at the wrong time? Explain.

_____

_____

_____

6. When Christine Martin needs to laugh, she often calls her sister or looks to her husband for some "comic relief." What makes you laugh? What enables you to temporarily set aside your problems and enjoy the emotional "medicine" of a good, old-fashioned belly roll? Do you laugh enough?

_____

_____

_____

7. Describe the people with whom you spend most of your spare time? Who are they? What are their priorities and driving beliefs? What do you talk about when you are with them? What does this tell you about yourself?

_____

_____

_____

8. Do you tend to be past oriented or future oriented? Explain. What do you normally do to move beyond the wounds and disappointments of the past?

_____

_____

_____

9. Briefly describe the most recent run-in you had with a friend, coworker, or family member. What caused the conflict? What do you think motivated the other person to resist you? How was the conflict resolved?

_____

_____

_____

10. Would you say that the image you have of yourself tends to be too high, too low, or just about right? What objective truth causes you to reach this conclusion? What can you do to change your self-image?

_____

_____

_____

DIGGING DEEPER

According to Christine Martin, the attitude you now exhibit is actually an acquired trait that can be "unlearned" and relearned the proper way. More than likely, your perspective on life was instilled in you by your family, friends, and environment and has been strengthened in your life by your own personal choices.

Can you trace your present attitude back to certain perspectives and beliefs that were instilled in you by your family and your environment? How did those factors contribute toward the attitude you now display?

_____

_____

_____

Are you able to see how your present attitude has been reinforced over time by your own beliefs and actions? Can you see how your friends have contributed to the solidification of your attitude? How have your own choices of words and friends contributed to the further entrenchment of your present attitude toward life?

_____

_____

_____

CHANGING HEARTS, CHANGING MINDS

*Do not conform any longer to the pattern of this
world, but be transformed by the renewing of your
mind. Then you will be able to test and approve
what God's will is—his good, pleasing and perfect will.*
Romans 12:2

God's plan of redemption actually requires three processes. The first process is salvation. Salvation is instantaneous and is based solely on faith. When a person comes to believe that Jesus is the Son of God and that he was raised from the dead, that person is saved. And once a person is saved, he or she cannot become any more saved. If a man should die five minutes after accepting Christ as his Savior, that man will be saved. If a woman should live 100 years after accepting Christ, that woman cannot become any more saved than she was the moment she first believed.

The third process in God's plan of redemption is resurrection. Through faith, God saves our souls. But the day will eventually come when he also will save our bodies from corruption. The resurrection is the ultimate fulfillment of the promises of God.

But in between salvation and resurrection, there is a second process of redemption that God is fulfilling in our lives. God is working to perfect us. He is working to teach us how to live out the faith that caused us to be saved. This is a lifelong process, and some people refer to it as "sanctification." But how does God change us? He changes us by changing our hearts so he can change our minds.

On the day you accepted Christ as your Savior, your heart was changed. That gave God a platform from which he could do the slow, tedious, lifelong work of changing your mind. And once your mind is changed, your behavior will change automatically. So the battle is in your mind, in the way you think, and that is where God desires to do his lifelong work of making us more like him.

God is smart. He knows that it is futile to try to change a person's thinking until the person's heart is changed. But with a new heart comes a hunger for a new way of thinking and a new way of looking at things and reacting to the people and circumstances around us. So thank God for your new heart. But now let the Holy Spirit use your new heart as a springboard to a new attitude, and let your new attitude catapult you to spiritual maturity and blessing.

SOMETHING TO THINK ABOUT

People tend to blame their feelings and problems on everything except their own poor attitudes.

People tend to blame their feelings and behaviors on their problems. But positive people have problems too. So how can you overcome the human tendency to wait until all your problems are solved before you can let yourself be happy?

_____

_____

_____

People tend to blame their feelings and behaviors on other people. But victorious people have to deal with the

same troublemakers you encounter every day. So how can
you deal with problem people and maintain a good attitude
at the same time?

_____

_____

_____

People tend to blame their feelings and behaviors on
external factors like their circumstances, their environment,
or even their genetic construction. But people with broken
families and past trauma often overcome these things to become happy and successful individuals. How can you overcome the negative influences in your life and rise above the
forces that have contributed to a negative attitude?

_____

_____

_____

MY PRAYER FOR A NEW ATTITUDE

Father, this is huge. I have come to realize that my attitude is everything. Like a compass, my attitude will point
me in the direction I will travel for the rest of my life. It will
propel me toward the destination I will reach with my life. So
I ask you, Lord, to give me a new attitude. I realize that my attitude has been instilled in me by many powerful forces over
many years of time. But I'm ready to begin the process today
of creating a new way of looking at life. So I ask you to help
me. I ask you to show me the way and to give me the resolve

and determination to "step out" of my old way of thinking and to "step in" to the new way you want me to view myself, others, and you. Help me begin this journey, and help me complete this journey. But also give me grace along the way so I can forgive myself for my past failures and keep going when things get difficult. With your help, I know I can make it. In Jesus' name, Amen!

MY SPIRITUAL JOURNAL

Take a few moments to record your thoughts regarding this week's session on a winning attitude. What new things did you learn? What new insights and revelations have you had? What life-changing truths did Christine Martin impart that have impacted your thinking? What changes will you make in the days ahead?

_____

_____

_____

FOOD FOR THOUGHT

The Bible describes God's Words as spiritual bread and spiritual meat. It is designed to nourish the spirit and the soul in the same way that food nourishes the body. So read the following scripture every day this week, repeating it out loud when you read it, and memorize it, if possible. And while you meditate upon this passage, make notes about anything you may observe about your personal life and any changes you may want to make.

Finally, brothers, whatever is true, whatever is noble, whatever is right, whatever is pure, whatever is lovely, whatever is admirable—if anything is excellent or praiseworthy—think about such things.
Philippians 4:8

_____

_____

_____

WISDOM FROM ABOVE

But the fruit of the Spirit is love, joy, peace, patience, kindness, goodness, faithfulness, gentleness and self-control.
Galatians 5:22-23

Do not lie to each other, since you have taken off your old self with its practices and have put on the new self, which is being renewed in knowledge in the image of its Creator.
Colossians 3:9-10

A joyful heart is good medicine, but a broken spirit dries up the bones.
Proverbs 17:22 (NASB)

COULD YOU REPEAT THAT?

Attitudes are like the flu: You "catch" attitudes from other people.

Refuse to dwell on the bad times of the past, and they will lose their power over you.

Life necessitates competition, and competition necessitates conflict.

IN A NUTSHELL

Your perspective on life is shaping the direction of your life.

CHAPTER 4:

An Orderly Life

If you hope to have an elevated spirit and a healthy outlook on life, you are going to need a reasonable amount of order in your life. Nothing can depress the human soul and deflate one's desire to do necessary things quite like disorder and chaos. But nothing can lift the human soul and boost one's passion for life quite like order and predictability.

When things are out of place in our lives, we become agitated and frustrated, and we tend to procrastinate when it comes to those things that require our attention. Our "to do" lists grow longer and longer as we continuously push things to tomorrow. But we push things to tomorrow because we see no reason to tackle them today. Everything else in our lives is a mess, so why should we bother addressing the issue that confronts us right now? Just throw it in the pile with everything else that needs to be organized, and we'll get around to it one of these days. Can you relate?

Take your closet, for instance. Your closet may be a small thing compared to the really important matters of life, but it is indicative of everything else. It needs some attention. For weeks your closet has been getting worse and worse, and now it is really starting to bother you. It is actually affecting the quality of your life. At first, your closet was slightly out of order and it was slightly annoying. But now you can't even function because you can't find anything. You have clothes scattered all over the bedroom floor and even in the living room and the back seat of your car. One of your shoes is in the closet, where it belongs, but the mate can't be found anywhere. Then one day, unexpectedly, you find it behind the washing machine in the utility room. How did it get there? It doesn't matter, I guess. All that really matters is that you desperately need some order in your life.

But once necessity actually forces you to clean and organize your closet, you feel better about yourself. You feel energized, productive, and complete. You also feel proud of yourself. How do I know? Because I'm just like you! And when I successfully tackle the mess, I proudly show my organized closet to my husband as soon as he returns home at the end of the day. So a little thing like an organized closet can change your self-image and lift your spirits. Somehow you found a way to rally the strength you needed to take on the chaos and to bring order to one small area of your life, and that small accomplishment changed you in a noticeable way. So just imagine what a clean house could do or a completely organized life.

If you want to keep organizing things after you arrange

your closet, I suggest you start with the smaller things in your life, the things you can finish relatively quickly, like your house. Crank up the music and get busy, just like you did when you attacked the closet. Music is the rhythm of the soul, so play some good music—some upbeat, catchy tunes—and get to work. Start feeling energized, and clean, clean, clean until the task is done. Make the bed, empty the dishwasher, scour the refrigerator, and empty the trashcans. Take action, and watch your spirit rise like a hot air balloon.

I don't know where you need order in your life. More than likely, if your closet is messy, your whole life is messy. But if the smaller things are in order, the more important things are probably in order, as well. A person tends to be either organized or disorganized, and this tendency seems to permeate every dimension of one's life. So to create order out of the chaos (the same way God did in the first chapter of Genesis), you should start with the smaller, simpler things. And I recommend starting with your house.

Why your house? Because your home is the place where you spend the most important hours of your day! Your home is the environment where you rest, recuperate, and interact with the most important people in your life. If your home is in order—spiritually and practically—you will be better equipped to engage all the chaos that confronts you every day in the rest of the areas of your life. Your mind and body will be healthier, your creativity will increase, and you will feel more emotional energy and stamina.

Please understand that I'm not trying to be mystical here. I'm not into New Age philosophy, and I'm not a practicing guru. I'm just telling you the truth from a practical standpoint. When you can easily find your backup jar of mustard and your red high heels, you will feel a whole lot better about yourself, your life will flow more smoothly, and you will feel comfortable and at ease in your own surroundings. And that will make a huge difference in your mental health, because your mind is an amazing thing. In the context of order and predictability, the human mind can do astounding things. But in the context of disorder and chaos, the mind starts to shut down.

Creating order in your life is a lot like creating a new attitude. You have to eat that elephant one bite at a time. But if you find a good starting place and then slowly, but methodically work your way out from the center toward the more remote parts of your life, you will find, over time, that you can make significant progress. You will find that, by moving one teaspoon full of dirt at a time, you can eventually relocate an entire mountain from here to there.

Personally, as I have stated, I think you need to start with your home, your haven. I think you need to create an environment where you can get away from the chaos so you will have the energy and resolve to tackle the more daunting areas of your disorganized life, one spoonful at a time. So clean your house, arrange your closets, organize the garage, and create a simple system in your cabinets so you can find your soup bowls and the chicken broth.

But don't stop with the obvious things. Organize your home by putting physical things in their appropriate places so your daily life can thrive, but also organize your home to create a peaceful environment where your family relationships can thrive. Set aside a specific time for family meals and a specific time for television. Create a time for family devotionals. Have established bedtimes, especially for the children. And control the music and other media that floods your house and affects your mood. Don't surrender your "castle" to invading forces. Take control of your own domain. If you can't manage the environment in your own home, how can you ever expect to manage the chaos that faces you in other sectors of your life?

Many families have established times to get up and to go to bed. Many families have established times for dinner, when they turn off the television and sit around the table to talk and to share a prayer. And many families have a tradition of going to breakfast together every Saturday morning as a family. But it doesn't matter what traditions you create. The point is: Start small and work your way toward bigger things. Start with the one or two areas that are causing you the most concern and work your way out from there. Do it slowly and gradually, giving your family time to adjust to each change before moving on to the next one. If you do, you will soon find that these simple changes can make a tremendous difference in your relationships and your personal life. Why?

Because order is a good thing and a reflection of the nature of God in our lives!

Also learn to create "systems" in your home. For instance, instead of running to the store every time you need a jar of mayonnaise, buy two jars of mayonnaise. Open one jar and place it in the refrigerator; then place the other jar on the "backup" shelf in your kitchen pantry. And teach the members of your family to write mayonnaise on the grocery list any time they take the last "backup" jar off the shelf. A little thing like this can help reduce chaos, because you will rarely find yourself making a special trip to the store for mayonnaise.

But don't stop there. File your receipts and paperwork, keep a family calendar somewhere in the house so every person can know the events that are coming up, and update your financial records every night or once a week. And instead of making a hair appointment for next Friday, go ahead and make all your hair appointments for the entire year so you won't have to worry about getting the time slot you want when you want it (and put all those appointments on the family calendar).

God created his universe to function with schedules and regularity. The earth rotates around the sun every 365 days, 6 hours. Water freezes at precisely 32 degrees Fahrenheit (every single time). The swallows return to the Mission San Juan Capistrano every year at early dawn on March

19th. And spring follows winter, which follows fall, when the leaves turn brown and the squirrels prepare for cold weather. Regularity and predictability make nature what it is. You, too, were created to have order in your life and to thrive in the presence of routine.

But don't make more out of this natural law than you need to. I am not saying that every activity should be pre-planned or that every action needs to be repeated every day in precisely the same way. Spontaneity is the spice of life. It is the unpredictable and unexpected things in life that create memories and lead to happiness. But 90 percent of what you do is repetitive. So why make life harder than it needs to be?

You know you are going to have to file your income tax returns on April 15th of every year. So why wait until April to start thinking about it? You know that Christmas is going to arrive every December 25th from now until the end of time, so why wait until the day after Thanksgiving to start digging for the money you need to buy gifts? Because of the natural human tendency to put things off, people fail to plan for retirement, they fail to set their affairs in order for their surviving relatives, and they fail to prepare for life's inevitable and repetitive events. But I am here to tell you that, if you can learn to organize and preplan just a few of the recurring things in your life, you will be amazed how much pressure that little bit of organization can take off you and how much time it can provide you to really enjoy the spontaneous moments that make life worth living.

The nature of God within us demands order. So if we repeatedly defy that inner call for order, we do harm to ourselves. We harm our balance, we harm our productivity, we harm our psychological health, we harm our reputations, and we harm our self-esteem. We place ourselves under an unnecessary pressure we were not created to bear, and we deny ourselves the happy hearts and elevated souls we so desperately crave.

So please! As you take steps to gradually and incrementally change your attitude, take similar steps to turn the disorder in your life into orderliness and structure. Begin at the center of your life by improving your home environment. Then from your organized home base, begin the process of addressing the other areas of your life that need to be more neatly arranged. And once you start the process, you will become addicted to order. Once you experience the benefits of an orderly life, you will become an organizational freak.

Once again, this is something I learned firsthand in my own life. One day, I looked into the mirror, and I did not like what I saw. I saw only disorder and chaos, confusion and frustration. From my closet to the deepest recesses of my heart, things were out of order, and my life was without discipline. So I decided to change. But once again, I didn't know where to start. So I did the same thing I had done when I decided to change my attitude. I started close to home and set out to move that mountain one spoonful of dirt at a time.

But before you take a look into your own mirror, I want you to know that it is not my intention to burden you with a lot of self-regulation. This book is about lifting your spirit, not crushing it beneath an unmanageable load of guilt. Too many rules can be worse than no rules at all, and the most burdensome rules are the rules we place upon ourselves in pursuit of perfection. So please don't fall into that trap. Don't become obsessed with order. On the other hand, if your life is out of order, do something to deal with the chaos. Take a small step forward to inject some sense of normalcy into your everyday life. If you don't, you're going to self-implode. Balance is what I'm recommending here. I want you to be healthy and happy, not a servant to chaos or excessive structure.

So take baby steps when you introduce new "systems" into your life. And take even smaller steps when you introduce new "systems" to your family. Not all your family members are like you, so give each member of your household room to be himself and to express his own personality. At the same time, however, all of you have to live together in harmony. What one member of the family does or fails to do will directly affect the other members of the household. So move forward deliberately in your pursuit of order, but move forward slowly.

Every great goal is achieved gradually, and every great dream is realized incrementally. The change from summer to winter, for instance, is a slow process as the temperature gradually changes and the plants and animals progressively respond. As a general rule, people don't go swimming one day and then start shoveling snow the next day. Likewise, your changes will be more effective and more enduring if you can take them slowly and work on them one at a time.

But somewhere along the line, you need to start focusing less on "urgent" things and start focusing more on the "important" things of life. The "tyranny of the urgent" is a condition that affects the quality of many people's lives and destroys many people's destinies and relationships. In the Western world particularly, we are so focused on the "urgent" things of life that we often neglect the more "important" things of life. Just think about it!

What is more important, your marriage or your job? Obviously, your marriage is more important. Even though your work may be important too, your job is merely a means to an end. You go to work every day so you can support and provide for your family. And your job could end tomorrow. There are no promises or guarantees when it comes to your employment. But your marriage is both a sacred trust and a personal responsibility that only you can honor. Only you can enhance your marriage and make it successful. And your marriage is a lifetime commitment.

So, if you are typical, you know you should invest substantial time in your marriage. You should think about the needs of your husband. You should arrange to spend time with your wife. You should plan special family getaways with your children. But then, far too often, those "important" plans are interrupted by an "urgent" situation at work. The computer system crashes or the alarm in the warehouse goes off, and it's your responsibility to attend to it.

That's okay once in a while. Stuff happens. But when the "urgent" situations at work become so routine and so disruptive that you have no time for your mate, that's a ticking time bomb waiting to explode. And the fact is that most of the emergencies can be eliminated with a little bit of forethought and some advanced planning. With a little bit of organization and creativity, a person can limit and control these kinds of "urgent" situations so he can focus more on the "important" matters of his life.

And that's what I'm talking about in this chapter. I'm not talking about adding more self-imposed regulations to your already packed schedule. I'm talking about creating systems and creating order that can help take some of the load off your shoulders and help you free up some of your time for the truly important things in your life. You need to spend some time with your children. You need to put some romance back in your marriage. You need to take a vacation without a cell phone or a laptop.

Before I understood the value of order in my life, here's the way a typical day would go for me: I might begin the day by setting out to clean my bathroom. But then, the phone rings, and I spend the next 30 minutes standing in the kitch-en, talking to my mom. I wouldn't consider this an interrup-tion: A conversation with my mother is one of those things I would regard as "important" in my life. But since I am now in the kitchen, my mind is focused on the kitchen. So, when I hang up the phone, I start cleaning the kitchen, and I forget about the bathroom.

Pretty soon, frustration sets in, because I have no sense of order and no sense of achievement. I have no plan for my day, so I don't know whether I have made progress or not. I just drift aimlessly from one task to another and from one urgent situation to the next. And then, before I know it, the day is over and I have nothing to show for my time. So I feel irritated, I feel unfulfilled, and I feel worthless.

But this is where baby steps can help, because now I ap-proach my day differently. Now, when I hang up the phone, I go back to the bathroom and pick up where I left off, because the bathroom stands at the top of my list of chores that I pre-pared the night before. And I prepared that list quite easily, because I know that my weekly routine calls for me to clean bathrooms on Tuesday, if possible. And after I clean the bath-rooms, the kitchen is next on my list.

So I have priorities for each day. I have a specific check-list of things that I want to achieve every day. And if I can somehow manage to finish all the projects on my list and take care of the unexpected things that will undoubtedly

arise throughout the day (the "urgent" things), I can actually
get a head start on Wednesday's projects so I will have time
to respond to the "important" opportunities that may spon-
taneously arise later in the week (or I can take some time off
for myself). And the opposite is true, as well: If an emergency
arises that keeps me from fulfilling my tasks on any given
day, I will have room in my schedule to get caught up later
in the week.

Having this kind of order in my life makes my life easier
to manage. In addition, it rewards me with a sense of purpose
and accomplishment. It also lifts my spirit. And even though
this approach to life's many responsibilities allows me to be
more productive and more fruitful, perhaps the greatest benefit of an organized life is that it allows me to be more flexible and spontaneous. On the surface this might sound like a
contradiction, but because of my organization and advanced
planning, I can talk with my mother for half an hour without feeling frustrated and I can join my husband for an unexpected lunch date without feeling guilty. I will have more
time for the "important" things of life and less fires to put out
if I will simply organize some of the routine aspects of my
life that currently demand so much of my time and attention.

In God's creation, we find perfect harmony between the
spontaneous and the predictable, between the expected and
the unexpected. While all maple leaves are similar, for instance, and while they all fall to the ground at the same time
of the year, no two maple leaves are exactly alike. And while

all the planets rotate on their axes and while they all orbit in the same direction around the sun, no two planets are exactly the same size, shape, or color and their atmospheres are all different.

God knows how to perfectly balance individuality and similarity, spontaneity and order. He knows how to blend impulse and constraint. When God created plants and animals, for example, he created all of them *"according to their various kinds"* (Genesis 1:11). In other words, every mouse carried a DNA code that enabled it to produce more mice, and every ginkgo tree bore seeds that allowed it to produce more ginkgo trees. But no two ginkgo trees are exactly alike, no two mice are exactly alike, and every human being has his own unique traits that set him apart from every other person on the face of the earth. So while every individual has red blood flowing through his veins and one heart that is positioned on the left side of his chest, no two people have the same fingerprints, the same retinal scan, or the exact same temperament or personality.

Order and design are not a threat to spontaneity and individuality. In fact, these qualities are complementary. They enhance one another. While impulse is essential to good mental health, orderliness is essential for creating and expressing non-destructive impulses. So organization actually sets you free and enhances your ability to enjoy life.

In addition, order is necessary for creating health and

balance in every imaginable aspect of your life. To be physically healthy, for example, you need to have some sort of plan in place for eating the proper foods and getting the exercise your body needs. If you just leave diet and exercise to the whims and fancies of your mood, your health will suffer in the long run.

As in every other aspect of your life, you need a "system" for eating if you plan to stay healthy. You need to know what you are putting in your body and how much of it you are putting there. If you don't, you will unknowingly migrate toward an undisciplined approach to eating, which will raise your cholesterol, add to your weight, and perhaps lead to diabetes or other health problems. The same is true with exercise. If you think you are going to naturally get the right kind of exercise and the right amount of exercise as you get older, you are just lying to yourself. You need some way to monitor, control, and discipline your physical activity as you create a regimen that assures proper physical health.

An orderly approach to life can definitely impact your health in a positive way, but an orderly approach to life can also enhance your family life by creating a peaceful environment where your spouse and your children can thrive because they have a more predictable and stress-free platform from which to engage life's challenges. An orderly approach to life can enhance your marriage by creating an atmosphere that is conducive to peace and tranquility rather than conflict and turmoil. And an orderly approach to life can enhance your financial wellbeing by creating a sense of control over your own money. At any given time, you will know exactly how much money you have and exactly how much money you need, and you will have a realistic plan for utilizing and distributing the financial resources that are at your disposal.

Personally, I don't think you can have order in the external things of your life unless you have order in the internal things of your life. If your personal life and your relationships are a disorderly mess, you are not likely to be an organized person when it comes to financial planning or housekeeping. But the opposite is true, as well. Internal order and external order seem to run hand in hand. And I don't guess it matters which one you establish first. Actually, it might be a good idea to address some aspects of both domains at the same time, because a chaotic environment can definitely create internal chaos, and internal chaos can definitely contribute to a lack of motivation for maintaining order in your surroundings.

So start with your home environment and go from there, but also work on prioritizing and organizing your personal life, starting with your relationship with God. Make sure that church attendance is a routine, not a special event. Make sure that prayer and Bible study are habitual, not occasional. And make sure that your giving is systematic, not haphazard. Regularity, even in your spiritual life, can create a sense of accomplishment that will enhance your self-image, fill you with a sense of peace, and establish a stable platform from which you can propel yourself into greater things.

But remember, it's all about baby steps. In the same way that the Christian life is a series of tiny steps forward (see Isaiah 28:13), so life is a series of tiny steps forward. In the same way that you learned to crawl, then stand, then walk, then run, and in the same way that you learned one word, then five words, then a hundred words, then thousands of words, so you must take small, yet continuous steps forward in your effort to manage your spiritual life, control your health, nurture your relationships, shape your home environment, give structure to your finances, arrange your work schedule, and systematize those repetitive routines that typically frustrate you to death.

If God is truly important to you, then you may want to stop approaching God on a hit-or-miss basis and you may want to start setting aside a regular time each day to pray, to sing, to rejoice, and to think about how far you have already come in your pursuit of an orderly life. At work, you may want to create a filing system for the growing pile of papers on your desk, or you may want to create a step-by-step timeline for finishing some of the projects that have been dumped in your lap. You may even want to devote some time each workday to nurturing your professional relationships so you can improve your work environment and your productivity. After all, people are like elevators: They will either take you up or take you down. They are like mathematics: They will either multiply, divide, add, or subtract from your life. So it is important to have order in your relationships so you can have order in your heart and mind. And this will lift your spirit.

But the point I am making here is that your list might be different from mine. In some areas, you may already be highly organized. In other areas, you might be poorly organized. In some areas, you may feel like you have a firm grip on life. In other areas, you might feel like the chaos has a firm grip on you. But the areas of life that need your attention are going to be different from the areas that need my attention, and your priorities will be unique to you. So start wherever you feel you need to start in order to bring order to your life, but please start somewhere. Start with those aspects of your life that are most powerfully impacting your mental health and do something to create more method and predictability in those vital arenas of your existence. Then move on to the next arena.

My job in this book is to give you information to enhance what you already know, to remind you of something you may have forgotten, and to help you see familiar truths from a new perspective. My responsibility is to inspire you and to motivate you to take action to make your life better. My task is to jump-start your engine so the Spirit of God within you can have a place to plant his feet as he initiates the changes in your life that are necessary for you to grow as a believer and a human being. But it's up to you to take action. It's up to you to decide whether you agree with me and what you should do to respond to the things I am telling you. It's up to you to think about the things I am saying and to craft your own response to the life lessons I am sharing with you here.

So while I have shared with you the discoveries of my life and the lessons I have learned during my journey from chaos to order and from confusion to clarity, I hope you will discover the areas of your own life where you can start creating your own unique type of order and start carving out a haven of peace and tranquility for yourself. If you want to lift your spirit, you need a place (both an emotional "place" and a literal place) where you can go to be restored and from which you can emerge with the strength to confront the challenges of life that await you.

Life is much sweeter where there is order. Life is more productive where there is order. Life is more rewarding and more gratifying and the issues of life are much easier to manage where there is order. Research proves that order contributes noticeably to a person's self-esteem and success. So make your bed. Organize your closet and your kitchen drawers. Buy a filing cabinet. Pick up an acrylic canister for your cotton balls or bath salts. Do whatever you need to do. But stop neglecting the chaos around you, and start doing something today to give method to your madness.

One of the fixed laws of God's creation is that any organized system left to itself will, in time, deteriorate into disorder and chaos; nothing will evolve into a more highly organized state without the direct intervention of an outside force. So stop neglecting the rising tide of disorder around you. Inject yourself into your own affairs and start creating order in your own little part of the world. You will be happier and healthier if you do, and the order you create will lift both your self-esteem and your spirit.

MODULE 4

AN ORDERLY LIFE

AN ORDERLY LIFE

1. Would you describe yourself as primarily "organized" or "disorganized"? Why do you view yourself this way? How do you think you got to be this way? Are you content with the amount of order that exists in your life? Do you think your organizational habits are consistent with your long-range goals?

_____

_____

_____

2. Does music stimulate you when you know you have work to do? What kind of music motivates you and helps you work?

_____

_____

3. When you walk into an extremely cluttered house, how does the environment affect you spiritually and emotionally? When you walk into a house that is well designed and spacious, how does that type of environment affect you? What does this tell you about yourself?

_____

_____

_____

4. Can you think of a large project that you finished slowly over time by moving one spoonful of dirt at a time? What was the project? How did you manage to complete the project incrementally? How did you feel when the project was finished?

_____

_____

_____

5. What are the "intangible" things (the unseen dynamics that create peace, harmony, and interaction) that need to be better organized in your home and family life? Which of these things stands at the top of your list of priorities? Why?

_____

_____

_____

6. Do you have a family calendar that is accessible to every member of the household? If not, how do you and the other members of your family coordinate and plan for all the office parties, ball games, and school events?

_____

_____

_____

7. How do you usually prepare for Christmas? When do you do your shopping? How do you plan your purchases and your holiday budget?

_____

_____

_____

8. What kind of things in your workplace tend to interfere with your personal plans and your family life? Is there any way you can better manage these emergencies in order to help you preserve your valuable time with the important people in your life?

_____

_____

_____

9. What is your "plan" for eating properly? Your "plan" for exercising? Do you have an actual "plan" for managing these important aspects of your life, or do you tend to take the path of least resistance?

_____

_____

_____

10. Every person must find the best possible starting point for introducing order to his or her life. Where will you start? What are the first few "baby steps" you will take to create order where chaos now rules in your life?

_____

_____

_____

DIGGING DEEPER

Christine Martin explains the necessity of differentiating between the "urgent" things of life and the "important" things of life. Urgent things, like fires, demand our immediate attention. However, the urgent things of life are not usually the most important things of life.

Describe two or three "urgent" things that often occur in your life. What makes these things urgent? How do they impact the truly important things in your life? What can you do to better manage these occurrences?

_____

_____

_____

Describe the two or three most important things in your life. Do you give adequate time and attention to these things? What distracts you from them? What can you do to remedy any imbalance that might exist in your life?

_____

THE CLIMATE OF THE HOME

She watches over the affairs of her household and does not eat the bread of idleness. Her children arise and call her blessed; her husband also, and he praises her.
Proverbs 31:28-29

Did you realize that the woman of the home creates the spirit of the home? God has appointed the man of the house as the prophet and priest of his home. He must represent the members of his family to God in prayer, and he must represent God to the members of his family through spiritual direction and example.

But while God holds the husband and father responsible for the spiritual direction of the family, he holds the wife and mother responsible for the spiritual climate of her home. In the final chapter of Proverbs, where the traits and qualities of a virtuous woman are clearly defined, we see a woman who is busy at home. She is busy in the marketplace, as well. But her primary responsibility is toward her family. Without her and the special abilities she brings, the family will suffer immensely.

Wives and mothers, if your home is out of order in any way—financially, logistically, operationally, financially, or spiritually—it is your assigned duty to bring order to the chaos and meaning to the madness. It is your responsibility to make your home both a delightful place to live and a constructive place from which your husband and children can launch into their destinies.

So do not eat the bread of idleness. Watch over the affairs of your household. If you do, your children will arise and call you blessed. Your husband will arise and praise you. And God will reward you tremendously, both now and throughout eternity.

SOMETHING TO THINK ABOUT

Introducing order to one's life is difficult and must be achieved slowly and incrementally. Introducing order to one's family is even more difficult, because each person is unique and the needs of each family member are unique.

Who is the most organized member of your family? How does this person's organization impact the family as a whole?

_____

_____

_____

Who is the most disorganized member of your family? How does this person's disorganization impact the family as a whole?

_____

_____

_____

In the past, how has your family managed to reconcile these two extremes? As you seek to introduce new "systems" of order to your family, how will the dynamic created by the diverse personalities within your family make your task easy? How will this dynamic make your task difficult?

_____

_____

_____

MY PRAYER FOR AN ORDERLY LIFE

Father, help me to organize my life. Help me to organize my home. Help me to organize the responsibilities that have been placed within my hands. Help me to organize the lives of those I love and serve. Show me where to start in my effort to bring order to disorder. Show me what to do. And help me to complete the journey once I start it. Give me patience and give me calm, so I can appreciate my life and enjoy it while I slowly bring it into alignment. And help me know what to arrange and what to leave alone. Don't ever let me become overbearing or too compulsive in my quest for tidiness. I want to be a blessing, Lord, not a curse. So help me to do what you did in the beginning when you put everything in its place and gave everything its purpose. In Jesus' name, Amen!

MY SPIRITUAL JOURNAL

Take a few moments to record your thoughts regarding this week's session on an orderly life. What new things did you learn? What new insights and revelations have you had? What life-changing truths did Christine Martin impart that have impacted your thinking? What changes will you make in the days ahead?

_____

_____

_____

FOOD FOR THOUGHT

The Bible describes God's Words as spiritual bread and spiritual meat. It is designed to nourish the spirit and the soul in the same way that food nourishes the body. So read the following scripture every day this week, repeating it out loud when you read it, and memorize it, if possible. And while you meditate upon this passage, make notes about anything you may observe about your personal life and any changes you may want to make.

So the word of the LORD to them will be, "Order on order, order on order, Line on line, line on line, A little here, a little there," That they may go and stumble backward, be broken, snared and taken captive.
Isaiah 28:13 (NASB)

_____

_____

_____

WISDOM FROM ABOVE

Now the earth was formless and empty, darkness was over the surface of the deep, and the Spirit of God was hovering over the waters. And God said, "Let there be light," and there was light.
Genesis 1:2-3

But all things should be done decently and in order.
I Corinthians 14:40 (ESV)

For whatever overcomes a person, to that he is enslaved.
II Peter 2:19 (ESV)

COULD YOU REPEAT THAT?

Nothing can depress the human soul and deflate one's desire to do necessary things quite like disorder and chaos.

Every great goal is achieved gradually, and every great dream is realized incrementally.

Order is necessary for creating health and balance in every imaginable aspect of your life.

IN A NUTSHELL

The nature of God within us demands order.

CHAPTER 5:

Spoil Yourself

I don't have to tell you that we live in a stressful world. In so many ways, the modern world is better than the world of yesteryear. I really like air conditioning, and I really like airplanes and cell phones. But for every technological advancement we have made over the centuries, we have surrendered a little bit of the simplicity of life. Today, things are faster and much more convenient. But with the help of our modern gadgets, we are moving at a faster pace, taking on more responsibilities, and trying to squeeze more activity into a typical day. So increased stress is an unintended consequence of our scientific advancement.

Very few people in the world have the convenience of locking themselves away from society. I occasionally read about some hermit who was discovered after living alone in a mountain cave for the past 20 years. But these kinds of events are as rare as a solar eclipse. Most of us have to live and work in a social framework that we cannot control. We have to function in a culture that moves at a blinding rate of speed.

So what do we do about the chaos? What do we do about the noise? What do we do about the busyness and the pressure and the fast pace of living? What do we do about the increased responsibility and the stress? As life grows increasingly complicated and increasingly problematic, how can we survive and flourish? How can we prosper in the midst of it all?

Generations ago, when the world was a simpler place, people didn't worry about stress as much as they do today. Things moved more slowly, and people moved more slowly. In addition, people spent most of their time doing hard physical work, which helps eliminate stress from the human body. There was no such thing as debt, because people paid for things as they went along. There was little concern about the bad news emerging from other parts of the world, because those things didn't really impact most Americans, and people usually didn't hear about these occurrences until they had ended.

But in today's world, where news travels at the speed of light and where constant danger lurks in the form of advanced technology, people are in tune with everything that is happening every minute of every day. And people are affected by everything that is happening, no matter where it occurs. All of us seem to be on the edge, and overwhelming forces are constantly pulling on us and our families. In this advanced, but demanding environment, it is absolutely necessary for people to take time for themselves. It is absolutely essential that each person take some time to withdraw from the constant bombardment of life's pressures and simply seek a place of solace.

Take time for "you." This is not a selfish thing; this is a necessary thing. God didn't intend for you to live at the pace you live. He didn't intend for you to function at the level you function. He didn't intend for you to carry this many balls and to haul this many buckets of water in a given day. You are not indestructible. If you don't listen to your own inner voice and to the cry of your own soul and your own body for rest, you won't last very long. And those who depend on you will suffer if you allow yourself to collapse under the pressure. So take some time to spoil yourself and to minister to your own needs. This will lift your spirit.

I am a natural-born "people watcher." I like to watch people, and I like to learn about human nature by noting the behaviors of those I observe. What I have learned over the years is that people are different. They are different in their mannerisms, different in their temperaments, and different in the way they do things and respond to their surroundings. But there is one constant that pervades the human experience: Every human being has exactly the same amount of time in a day, a week, a month, or a year. But in the same amount of time, one person can do twice as much as another person. In the same amount of time, one person can go twice as far as another person. In the end, each person has the same amount of time in a day or a week. But while some people squeeze a lot out of that time, other people squeeze very little out of that same amount of time, because it's not the amount of time we have, but what we do with our allotted time that determines the quality of our lives.

So I choose to take some of that time for myself. I don't want to become so busy with life that I miss life altogether. I don't want to work so hard selling photographs of sunsets that I never take the time to actually look at a real sunset. And I don't want to spend so much time accumulating beautiful things that I never take a day to just walk through a national park to enjoy the beauty of God's creation.

I cannot withdraw from a bank account what I have never deposited into that account, and I can never withdraw from life what I have never deposited into life. So I want to take the time to enjoy my life and to enjoy my family and God's creation, and I want to take the time to enjoy all the other truly meaningful things that God gave to man when the world moved more slowly and when life was much simpler and more focused on things of substance. I want to invest in real life. I don't want to get sucked into the fast-paced spirit of this age.

But if it's going to be, it's up to me. It's up to me to create priorities in my life that will draw protective boundaries around my precious time. It's up to me to safeguard my own sanity and my inner peace. It's up to me to say "no" to all the distractions and opportunities the world will offer me every day. It's up to me to choose instead to take time for the things that actually matter and can genuinely enrich my life. I have to organize my time. I have to protect my time. I have to demand time for myself. I have to turn off all the electronics and all the unnatural connections with the outside world and withdraw from the pressures of life in order to be refreshed, rejuvenated, and restored. I have to plant hedges of protection around my life and my time.

The greatest thing about life is also the worst thing about life: Life is a series of choices. I get to choose my mate. I get to choose my career. I get to choose where I live. I get to choose my friends. I get to choose what I eat, what I wear, what I drive, and what I watch. But with every choice, there is a resulting consequence. And that is where life gets complicated.

As human beings, we want it all. We want everything that life can offer us. We want to sample everything at least once. And we want to move on from that experience to every other experience that life can offer us. But we don't want to pay the invoice for this morning's choices and yesterday's behaviors. And that is where life gets dicey, because God will never repeal the everlasting law of the universe that *a man reaps what he sows*" (Galatians 6:7). Consequently, I am forced to choose. I can't do it all. I can't have it all. There's not enough money, there's not enough time, and there's not enough of "me" to go around.

So for everything I want from life, I must learn to say

"no" to thousands of other offers. If I want a husband, I must say "no" to every other man who could be a potential mate. If I want a career, I must say "no" to every other professional endeavor that is out there for the taking. If I want a family, I must say "no" to the independent and carefree lifestyle that I enjoyed when I was younger. If I want wealth, I must say "no" to my current desire to spend the money in my hand. And if I want tranquility, I must learn to prioritize my life and say "no" to a lot of things that would consume my time and place more responsibility on my shoulders than I really ought to bear.

There is a price tag associated with every choice I make, and it is easy to buy into too many things that life dangles before me. Therefore, in this modern world, where the options are plenteous and where merchandisers tell me I can have it all, I must learn to focus on those few things that really matter to me and I must pour myself into those important things while rejecting all the other distractions of life, although those distractions glisten with appeal and call to me from afar with the lure of a mythological siren.

God is the most important thing in life. My family comes next and then my destiny. But while God, my family, and my destiny add to my life, they also subtract from my life in the sense that they require my time, my energy, my effort, and my resources. And there is only so much of me to go around. So if I intend to stick around for the people and things that truly mean something in my life, I must protect my own sanity. I must take care of myself for the sake of my God and my husband and my son and my ministry. I must carve out a portion of every day just for myself, so I can vacate all the requirements and resulting stress that life's demands place upon me. And when I do, there will be more of me to go around in the long run.

It is so important to have "down time." Cars need gas and kids need food if they intend to keep running at high speeds. You, too, need some "down time" to fuel your engine and recharge your battery. In fact, God, who designed us in the first place, tells us that we need time for ourselves. He tells us through his Word and he tells us through his creation that rest and recuperation are absolutely necessary to health and to life.

In the Bible, for instance, God set an example for us when he rested after the work of creation (see Genesis 2:1-2). When God finished creating the heavens and the earth, he set aside an entire day for physical rest. And later, he would make the practice of weekly rest a mandatory requirement for his covenant people (see Exodus 20:8).

But the Bible doesn't stop with a call for physical rest; the Bible also speaks frequently about spiritual rest. For instance, Jesus said, *"Come unto me, all you who are weary and burdened, and I will give you rest"* (Matthew 11:28). And the author of Hebrews tells us, *"Anyone who enters God's rest also rests from their works"* (Hebrews 4:10). So even God commissions us to seek rest. He commissions us to seek rest from our demanding physical responsibilities, and he commissions us to seek rest for our souls from the human tendency to work for his approval and love.

But God goes a step farther by giving us various pictures through nature of the value of rest. The bear, for instance, hibernates during the most stressful season of the year. He (or she) decides to simply relax and wait for the ordeal of winter to pass rather than work extra hard to combat it. And the butterfly uses a time of rest to transition from one state to another. Before the slow and slimy caterpillar can turn into the fast and beautiful buttery, the caterpillar must bury itself within a cocoon to rest during a certain period of its life. Whether it wants to or not, the caterpillar is forced to rest, and that rest results in resurrection to a whole new existence.

When we are rested, it shows. When we are rested, we perform better, we think better, and our attitudes are easier to accommodate. When we are rested, people can really tell. They also can tell when we are stressed out, because people who are overloaded and under-rested tend to be grumpy, grouchy, irritable, and unreasonable. They tend to be confrontational, angry, and shortsighted while those who are refreshed in body and soul tend to make good decisions, speak words of life, and look on the bright side of things. We especially treat our loved ones better when we are rested and revitalized.

If you are feeling frazzled and if you are getting less sleep than you need, the stress is piling up on your body and your brain. And one day soon, you're going to explode. If you are running here and there and if you are feeling like you are getting farther behind rather than farther ahead, you will only be able to absorb the pressure for so long. And if you have placed too many demands on yourself and too much of you is being scattered in too many directions, you are a disaster waiting to happen. Your stress is too high, and your resistance is too low. You were not designed to live like this; you need to take some time for yourself.

A generation ago, most people would have skipped a chapter about rest. But today, rest is the one thing that everybody needs. Modern life is pushing all of us to the limit, and more people are breaking beneath the weight than ever before. Road rage is out of control. Violent crime is on the rise. Domestic violence is at an all-time high. Drug and alcohol use are soaring as people seek relief from their problems. And suicide—even teenage suicide—is at epidemic levels.

People just can't take it anymore. Something has to give. And even though I would encourage you to find a long-term solution to your stress problem by establishing priorities for your time and eliminating a lot of unnecessary things from your schedule, I am concerned right now about your immediate, short-term relief. Until you can take full inventory of your life and rearrange your goals accordingly, I want you to learn to relax. I want you to learn to seize the moment to enjoy life and to breathe in the wonderful oxygen of God's creation. Don't wait until you're at the end of your rope. Don't wait until exhaustion puts you in the hospital. Learn to find some time here and there—every single day—to unwind and relax.

During the middle of your busy day, slip away for lunch with your husband or a friend. During the middle of your busy day, take a 20-minute nap. We make kids take naps. When did we stop following our own advice to our children? Set aside a little time every day for something that is purely enjoyable and relaxing. And even if you have to eliminate something more productive from your regimen, a segregated time of rest will actually prove to be more beneficial in the long run.

So take an hour each day just for yourself. Take a day each week. Take a couple of weeks each year. Take an entire year once or twice during your lifetime. And during your time off, do something that will completely take your mind off your problems and responsibilities. Watch an old movie. Soak in a hot tub while listening to some soothing music. Or just sit in the back yard and watch the sun set behind the trees while the birds compete for the top position on the telephone wire. Listen to the crickets and the frogs in the distance, and watch the stars emerge in the sky until the mosquitoes make it impossible to stay. And sip slowly on that ice-cold tea until the condensation from the glass forms a puddle on the patio table.

Whatever floats your boat is fine with me. Whatever quivers your liver! But please, do something every day, every week, every year to make sure you get the rest you need and to make sure you control the stress levels in your body and your mind.

Most people think that their circumstances dictate their beliefs. But I know that a person's beliefs dictate his circumstances. For instance, if you believe that you can, then you probably can. If you believe that you can't, then you probably can't. No matter what you believe, you're right. And the same is true when it comes to time. If you believe you don't have any time to do these necessary things, then you don't. But if you believe you can make the time, then you can. If you believe that time controls you, then it does. But if you believe that you control your time, then you do. And if you believe that time is the most important commodity that God has entrusted to you, then you will use your time wisely and find a way to better organize the most precious commodity God has placed in your hands.

Time seems to be flexible too, and this is another enigma of life. Time stretches or shrinks to fit our expectations of it. Just think about this for a moment!

When you were in high school and your teacher gave you an assignment to write a research paper that would come due the last day of the semester, when did you finally finish your work on that project? That's right! You finished your term paper the night before it was due. In fact, you were probably making last-minute changes to it while the teacher was taking up the papers. She gave you the assignment in January and the report wasn't due until May. But you managed to take all that time to complete the project, because the time was available.

But here's the mystery of time: If your teacher had given you just one week to complete the assignment, you still would have finished the project the night before it was due and you still would have been making final corrections while the teacher was taking up the papers. If you have a lot of time to complete a task, you will take a lot of time to do it. But if you have very little time to complete a task, you will find a way to do it in the time that is allotted to you. Time is elastic, and it has a way of stretching or shrinking to fit the need.

In the end, however, time is of the essence. It is the most important possession at our disposal. At the end of your life, when you are gasping for your final breath of air, you won't be wishing that you could buy another car. You won't be wishing that you could put new flooring in your house. You won't be wishing that you could go to work just one more time or that you could have just one more winning trade on the stock market. None of these things will mean anything to you as the end of your life approaches. But if you are like most people, you would be willing to do almost anything for a few more moments of time.

This is why God instructed Paul to redeem the time (see Ephesians 5:16). Treat it with respect. Treat it with reverence. Value time highly, and squeeze the most out of it that you possibly can squeeze, because, unlike all other commodities, time cannot be stored away for future use nor can it be held until a rainy day. Time must be consumed every second of every minute of every hour of every day until it is finally gone and eternity begins. So spend it well. Spend it wisely. Spend it with prudence and with wisdom, because, when it is used, it cannot be retrieved, and there are no "do overs" when it comes to time.

All you really have is today. When tomorrow finally arrives, it won't be "tomorrow" anymore. It will be called "today." So *this is the day the Lord has made; let us rejoice and be glad in it*" (Psalm 118:24). Even though you must be a faithful steward by investing a lot of your time in your responsibilities and in your own survival, don't let all your time slip away without enjoying the rich things of life, things like a mountain sunrise or an ocean sunset, things like the first flowers of spring or the crisp autumn air against your skin. Don't let your life evaporate a day at the time without relishing the truly wonderful things that God has placed around you. Don't work and worry yourself to death. Enjoy your mate. Enjoy your children and your grandchildren. Laugh, smile, go for a walk, and talk to the people you love. Take care of business, but don't let business become more important than it should. In the end, all that will really matter to you is God, the people you love, and your legacy.

When it came to the subject of time, Jesus taught a life-style of balance. On the one hand, he said, "As long as it is day, we must do the work of him who sent me" (John 9:4). So obligations are important, and one's purpose in life is important, too. But Jesus also said, "Do not worry about tomorrow, for tomorrow will worry about itself" (Matthew 6:34). So we must learn to relax and to enjoy life along the way. We must not let all the cares and problems of life rob us of the things that truly matter. There will be problems every day and most of them can wait an hour or two while we take some reasonable time for ourselves. But if we don't learn to control our problems, our problems will eventually control us and will steal every irreplaceable moment and every precious memory from us as we focus on the "urgent" things of life and never get around to the truly "important" things.

There are lots of books on the market that can give you some great ideas on how to unwind and relax. But let me give you just a couple of ideas that have worked well for me over the years.

First of all, learn to say "no" to your telephone, especially at night when you are at home with your family. If you don't feel like spending your "down" time on the phone, just refuse to answer it when it rings. After all, this person is calling you without your permission. Remember? The caller obviously wants to talk, but that doesn't mean that you have to spend your relaxation time talking to him. Especially in this day and age of caller ID, you can make an informed decision whether to take a particular call. But here's my suggestion: If the call could involve a distraction or another one of those never-ending "emergencies," consider skipping the call and dealing with it later. Very few interruptions involve life-and-death situations that can't wait for your attention.

Another thing you can do to help yourself relax is to keep a journal of your thoughts and your daily progress. For some people, journaling is work. But for me, it's relaxing. Writing helps me release what is bottled up inside me, and it helps me enhance my thoughts and feelings. And nobody can judge me when I write (unless I choose to share my writings with another person). It's just me and my thoughts. So think about finding a quiet place where you can record your thoughts for today and review your thoughts from yesterday. And as you read over the things you wrote last week and last month, be encouraged by the progress you are making and the goals you are achieving.

In closing, let me quickly list a few more things you can do to relax and to soak up all the wonder that life has to offer. These things may seem simple, but that's the point. The most wonderful things in life are the simple things.

1. Walk around the mall just for fun. You don't have to buy anything; you can just window shop. Of course, it doesn't always work out that way, so I wouldn't recommend this type of relaxation therapy if you happen to be a compulsive shopper. You want to rest, and you want your wallet to rest, too. But if you can avoid spending money impulsively and just

enjoy the scenery and the people, this is an excellent way to clean out all the cobwebs and rest your mind.

2. Walk down memory lane. Take out some old photos of you or your family and reminisce about the fun times you've had and the fun places you've experienced.

3. Take a bubble bath. Obviously, this one's for the women, but men can do this too (I promise I won't tell). Turn off the phone, put on some soothing music (maybe light some candles), and just float away into your own personal paradise.

4. Schedule a lunch date with your husband or wife or perhaps an old friend or someone else whose company you enjoy. Eat at the nicest restaurant you can afford. A lunch getaway can provide a great midday break from your normal routines and can help you reconnect with somebody you love. And there's another great benefit to lunch: You can eat at the nicest restaurants for less money, because lunch is a lot less expensive than dinner.

5. If you tend to be healthy in your eating habits and if you usually exercise, grant yourself one day each week to indulge. Then take that day and go to an ice cream parlor or a candy shop or some other place where you can reward yourself with the treats you typically avoid. And don't punish yourself later for your leniency. Remember, this is an indulgence, not a lifestyle.

6. Rent a movie and just "veg out" at home all night with a big bowl of popcorn and your favorite blanket.

7. Just say "no." You don't have to accept every invitation that comes your way. The more time you save, the more rest and relaxation you're going to get. And the less you spread yourself around, the more you will be able to effectively give of yourself to those who truly matter.

8. Visit a nursing home, a homeless shelter, or some other place where you can give some of your time to others in a way that is different for you. This will refresh you in a surprising way and simultaneously reward you with a sense of satisfaction, because you will know that you selflessly gave away some of your irretrievable time to another human being who desperately needed it.

These are just a few ideas. But you can come up with ideas of your own that better fit your personality and your particular circumstances. Yet regardless of what you choose to do, please understand how important it is to use your time wisely and to your advantage. And never forget how necessary it is to regroup, relax, and rejuvenate every day, every week, and on special occasions you have set aside throughout the year. Life is difficult and it is growing more difficult with every rising generation. So take charge of your time and take charge of your life. Spoiling yourself just a little bit can definitely lift your spirit.

MODULE 5

SPOIL YOURSELF

SPOIL YOURSELF

1. What things matter most to you in life?

_____

_____

_____

2. Are there certain behaviors you exhibit when you are tired and stressed? How can those closest to you tell when you are well rested and when you have pushed yourself too hard?

_____

_____

_____

3. Do you currently have too much stress in your life? What are the sources of your stress? What can you do to relieve some of the undue stress derived from these activities?

_____

_____

_____

4. Christine Martin focused primarily on short-term solutions to the problem of stress. What specific things can you do long-term to lower the stress levels in your life?

_____

_____

_____

5. What completely takes your mind off your problems and responsibilities? Do you tend to engage in this activity too often or not often enough? What can you do to enjoy this pleasurable activity in a balanced way?

_____

_____

_____

6. Do you believe that time controls you, or do you believe that you control your time? Explain.

_____

_____

_____

7. What are the three wisest investments of your time that you typically make? What are the three poorest investments of your time?

_____

_____

_____

8. Are you the kind of person who worries or the kind of person who tends to look on the positive side of things? Does your temperament add to your stress or help relieve it?

_____

_____

_____

9. When you are at home at night, relaxing with your family, how do you typically respond to an incoming phone call? Why?

_____

_____

_____

10. Do you normally consider your invitations carefully, or do you instinctively accept most invitations for activities outside your home? How do you feel about your social life and its benefits or toll upon your life?

_____

_____

_____

DIGGING DEEPER

Christine Martin explains that it is up to each of us to create priorities in our lives that can create a healthy balance between responsibility and relaxation.

What protective boundaries have you established to protect your precious time? What new boundaries do you believe you need to establish to safeguard your sanity and your inner peace?

_____

_____

_____

What distractions does the world routinely place in your path to steal your time? What "opportunities" have you recently encountered that have the potential of creating new stress in your life? What criteria do you weigh as you consider whether to accept or reject these "opportunities"?

_____

_____

_____

THE CLIMATE OF THE HOME

Anyone who enters God's rest also rests from their works, just as God did from his. Let us, therefore, make every effort to enter that rest....
Hebrews 4:10-11

In order to convey the absolute necessity for physical rest, God instituted the weekly Sabbath and declared it to be a sacred and holy day on the Jewish calendar. But the writer of Hebrews makes it clear that the concept of the Sabbath extends beyond physical rest. The writer also makes it clear that people must learn to rest "spiritually" in order to adequately observe the Sabbath principle.

The word sabbath means "to cease and desist." So the very word itself has a connotation of resting from all labor. In the physical sense, God wants his people to set aside regular times to cease and desist from their work, as he did after the six days of creation. And he wants his people to be physically and emotionally restored as they sit back to enjoy what their hands have created and as they appreciate what God created with his hands.

But the writer of Hebrews also makes it clear that God wants us to cease and desist from our spiritual labor. Too many people are too busy trying to impress God. Through good works, through incessant service that interferes with their God-given responsibilities, and through excessive self-denial, they try to earn God's favor and his love. But the very definition of grace demands that we rest from our spiritual works and allow God's love to fill in the blanks that we cannot fill ourselves.

So enter God's rest. Rest from your labors, and *rest in the Lord, and wait patiently for him*" (Psalm 37:7, KJV). You will be more fulfilled and satisfied if you do.

SOMETHING TO THINK ABOUT

The world is changing at an unbelievable pace. But according to Christine Martin, for every technological advancement we have made over the years, we have surrendered a little of the simplicity of life. Today, things are faster and more convenient. But because of these changes, we are moving at a faster pace, taking on more responsibilities, and trying to squeeze more activity into a typical day.

What is the most significant cultural or technological change you have noticed in society over the course of your lifetime?

_____

_____

_____

What has society gained as a result of this change?

_____

_____

_____

What do you believe society has lost in exchange for this advancement?

_____

_____

_____

MY PRAYER FOR REST

Father, teach me balance in my life. You told me to work while it is day. But you also told me to honor the Sabbath day and to rest from my works. I don't want to be lazy, but I don't want to overwork either. So give me your wisdom. Give me your balance so I can honor all your commands and live the kind of productive and fulfilling life that you destined me to live. I thank you, Lord, that you have given me responsibilities in life. Help me to be a good steward and to honor you as I fulfill my obligations. But also help me to remember what is truly important and to maintain the priorities you have established for me in your Word. Help me to rest from my labors. And, as I do, restore my soul and replenish my strength. In Jesus' name, Amen!

MY SPIRITUAL JOURNAL

Take a few moments to record your thoughts regarding this week's session on spoiling yourself. What new things did you learn? What new insights and revelations have you had? What life-changing truths did Christine Martin impart that have impacted your thinking? What changes will you make in the days ahead?

_____

_____

_____

FOOD FOR THOUGHT

The Bible describes God's Words as spiritual bread and spiritual meat. It is designed to nourish the spirit and the soul in the same way that food nourishes the body. So read the following scripture every day this week, repeating it out loud when you read it, and memorize it, if possible. And while you meditate upon this passage, make notes about anything you may observe about your personal life and any changes you may want to make.

Remember the Sabbath day by keeping it holy. Six days you shall labor and do all your work, but the seventh day is a Sabbath to the Lord your God. On it you shall not do any work, neither you, nor your son or daughter, nor your male or female servant, nor your animals, nor any foreigner residing in your towns. For in six days the Lord made the heavens and the earth, the sea, and all that is in them, but he rested on the seventh day. Therefore the Lord blessed the Sabbath day and made it holy. (Exodus 20:8-11)

_____

_____

_____

WISDOM FROM ABOVE

Come unto me, all you who are weary and burdened,
and I will give you rest.
Matthew 11:28

Be very careful, then, how you live—not as unwise but
as wise, making the most of every opportunity, because the
days are evil.
Ephesians 5:15-16

This is the day the Lord has made; let us rejoice and be
glad in it.
Psalm 118:24

COULD YOU REPEAT THAT?

For everything I want from life, I must learn to say "no" to thousands of other offers.

It is so important to have "down time."

In the end, all that will really matter to you is God, the people you love, and your legacy.

IN A NUTSHELL

I want to invest in real life. I don't want to get sucked into the fast-paced spirit of this age.

CHAPTER 6:

Mirror, Mirror On the Wall

Unless you were raised on Mars, you're well aware of the classic Bavarian fairy tale, Snow White. In 1937, Walt Disney made a full-length animated film about this famous tale, and all of us remember that captivating scene where the wicked queen peered into the magical mirror and asked the all-important question: "Mirror, mirror on the wall, who's the fairest of them all?" This scene clearly portrays the importance of image and the way we appear to others and ourselves.

In fact, vision is an amazingly powerful force—perhaps the most powerful of all the five senses—because, through the eye, we gain most of our perspective on life. How we view the things around us or interpret our circumstances is often determined by what we see with our eyes. So how do you see yourself? Do you see yourself through the eyes of God, or do you have a poor self-image? Do you see the person God created you to be, or do you see what others have declared you to be? When the queen presented her question to the magical mirror, she wanted to know if the mirror truly saw what she saw.

Obviously, there's no such thing as a magical mirror. So when you and I look into a mirror, we see what's really there. But the way we interpret what we see determines everything about us. It determines the course of our lives, the quality of our lives, and the outcome of our lives. It determines the kind of day we will have and the kind of future. The person who sees something bad in the mirror is the person who will usually engage each event of his life from a negative starting point while the person who sees something good is the person who will engage things from a positive perspective.

People tend to view themselves in one of three ways. First, people view themselves as other people see them. In other words, some people choose to define themselves the way that other people define them. This can be good if people tend to see you as a person of great worth and potential, but most of the time the appraisal of others can be cruel, inaccurate, and restrictive. Over the course of your life, most of the people who give you their assessment of your value will project onto you the limitations they see for themselves. They will restrict you on the basis of the past failures they have experienced in their own lives.

Second, people tend to view themselves through their own eyes. Once again, this can be positive or negative, depending on the appraisal a person holds of his own true worth. Unfortunately, most of those who have helped us shape our attitudes about ourselves are people who have limited expectations of life and limited exposure to true greatness. Consequently, most of us grow up with less than healthy assessments of ourselves, because we have been fed a constant diet of negativity about our own worth.

The third and the best way to view oneself is through the eyes of God. To see yourself the way God sees you is the only accurate way to grasp your true identity and potential. According to the Bible, God sees you "in Christ." In other words, he sees you the same way he sees his Son, Jesus. He sees you complete and perfect, the way you will be when he finishes all his gracious work in your life.

But regardless of where you fall on this scale of self-analysis, this much is certain: The way you see yourself makes a world of difference in the way you live your life and the way you feel about yourself. It makes a world of difference in the way you view God, the way you treat others, and the way you approach the future and interpret the past. Your self-image shapes your beliefs, your values, your priorities, and your relationships. It determines the way you spend your time and your money. It controls the outcome of your life.

When you see true value in yourself, you attract more goodness into your life. You attract personal happiness from within, and you attract good people from without. You encourage good friendships, and you create good endings. So you should appreciate who you are. But alas! That is the challenge, isn't it?

Very few people have adequate appraisals of themselves and their own worth. Even the Bible seems to insinuate that people fall into three categories when it comes to self-analysis. To capitalize on another famous fairy tale, let's face the fact that there are a lot of people out there who think too highly of themselves (too hot), there are a lot of people who think too lowly of themselves (too cold), and there are a few blessed individuals who think properly about themselves (just right). So let's briefly analyze these three biblical attitudes toward "self" so we can better understand the distorted self-images that the Bible warns us about and the wholesome self-image that the Bible promotes.

Obviously, the Bible has a great deal to say about pride, the tendency to think too highly of oneself. There is no shortage of people who think of themselves too highly. In fact, the Bible seems to indicate that pride was the original sin. According to Isaiah 14:12-17, pride was the underlying motivation that led to Lucifer's downfall. It was an inflated view of himself that somehow convinced the angelic cherub that he was equal with the Almighty and that he could successfully defy the God who created him. And once pride took root in Lucifer's heart, he stirred up discontentment among some members of the heavenly host, apparently taking advantage of the same tendency in them toward pride. Together, these haughty creatures engaged in conspiracy and an attempted overthrow of the sovereignty of the Lord. But when the rebellion failed, Lucifer (who became known as Satan) carried his rebellion to the earth, where he approached Eve and deceived her through her prideful tendencies.

King Solomon noted that *"pride goes before destruction, a haughty spirit before a fall"* (Proverbs 16:18). In other words, pride and arrogance, egotism and haughtiness, are the root cause of every sin and every spiritual malady. When a person fails to recognize his own limitations and starts to view himself as immortal, infallible, and unaccountable to his creator and others, that person has crossed the line and is destined for destruction.

Pride is understandable among the unbelievers of the world. After all, if they don't elevate themselves, who will? But pride also seems to be an ongoing problem among the people of God, just as it was a problem for the angels of heaven. In fact, the apostle Paul was forced to address the problem of pride when he wrote to the believers in Rome. He told them, *"Do not think of yourself more highly than you ought"* (Romans 12:3). So Paul was forced to draw a line on self-esteem, even for God's people. He was compelled to draw a line and warn the people not to cross it by elevating themselves excessively in their own minds.

It is important to note that the "line" Paul drew was the line of reality and sane thinking. Paul told the Christians in Rome not to get carried away with their own appraisal of themselves. But this is extremely important: Paul did not tell the believers in Rome to think of themselves lowly. He did not tell them to deplore themselves or despise themselves or berate themselves or put themselves down. He did not tell them to compensate for their prideful tendencies by putting on a cloak of false humility and flogging themselves while they sat in sackcloth and ashes. He simply drew a reasonable line and told them not to cross it.

Paul told the Christians at Rome that it was okay for them to think of themselves highly, but he told them not to think of themselves "more highly than you ought." In other words: "You should think as highly of yourself as God thinks of you, and he thinks very highly of you. Consequently, you should walk with your head high and your shoulders erect. You should walk in confidence and with resolve. You should walk in assurance and in strength of conviction. But you should never cross the line where you start thinking that you are bigger and smarter and better than you really are. You should never cross that line and start thinking that you are invincible or infallible or above rebuke. After all, you are made of dust, you are saved by grace, and you are a servant to the one who created you. So don't let your head swell.

Excessive pride, therefore, seems to be the biggest malady of the human heart whether we are talking about believers or unbelievers. But there are lots of people out there who have the opposite problem. There are lots of people who think too lowly of themselves. Moses thought too lowly of himself when God called him to be his representative to Pharaoh (see Exodus 3:7-4:14). Gideon thought too lowly of himself when God called him to lead Israel in battle against the Midianites (see Judges 6:11-16). Jeremiah thought too lowly of himself when God called him to be a prophet to Judah (see Jeremiah 1:4-7). And Saul thought too lowly of himself when God sent the prophet Samuel to anoint him as the first king of Israel (see I Samuel 9:19-21).

So the problem of low self-esteem seems to be almost as prevalent in the Bible as the problem of excessive pride. But the point of the biblical text is that God doesn't want us to think of ourselves too highly (too hot) or too lowly (too cold). Instead, God wants us to think of ourselves "just right." He wants us to see ourselves the way he sees us. He wants us to realize that we have our own individual strengths and our own human limitations. He wants us to realize that we all have past failures and future potential. God sees us as cleansed. He sees us as forgiven. He sees us as precious and as having immense value. But God doesn't see us as worthy of adoration.

God also wants each of us to know that we have something to contribute that nobody else can contribute. The Bible clearly teaches that each person has at least one talent that other people lack and that each person's destiny is usually discovered by making that unique talent available to others. But while each person has at least one talent or ability to offer to others, no person has everything. So we all need one another, and God designed his kingdom that way to keep us humble while confirming our individual worth.

Where is this explained in the Bible? In I Corinthians 12, Paul devotes the entire chapter to the explanation of this concept. First, he explains that each believer has a special "gift" to contribute to the other members of the family of God (see I Corinthians 12:1-31). Then Paul uses the analogy of the human body to help us see that we do indeed possess at least one valuable quality that is intended to benefit others.

Paul compares one member of the church to the human ear and another member of the church to the human eye. Utilizing the analogy of the human body, Paul makes it clear that some people are able to do what other people cannot do in the same way the ear is able to do what the eye cannot do. Drawing a very vivid word picture, Paul instills worth in each member of the church, making it clear that the small contribution of each person is necessary for the overall health of the body. But then Paul tempers this explanation of individual worth with a healthy balance of humility. He shows how the ear needs the eye and how the eye needs the ear. He also explains how the less glorified parts of the human body tend to receive less recognition (like the feet), but that these parts of the body are actually the more important parts (see I Corinthians 12:22).

This explanation of a balanced perception of oneself is extremely important to one's spiritual health, but sometimes the Bible makes its points more forcefully through real-life examples than through doctrinal instruction. Consequently, I like the way that this same concept is taught to us implicitly through the narrative portions of the Bible. And one of my favorite narratives on this subject is the story of Bezalel and Oholiab.

Bet you never heard of these two guys! Nevertheless, they are important figures in the biblical epic. Where can you read about them? In Exodus! Do you remember when God appeared to Moses on Mount Sinai and gave Moses this really long and detailed description of a tabernacle that he wanted Moses to build for him? The book of Exodus goes on and on about the details for the curtains and the pegs and the ropes and the utensils that would make this tabernacle the most awesome place possible for the Israelites to worship God. So God gave this amazing vision to Moses for this wonderful "house" where the Lord would abide among his people.

But Moses didn't know how to build this tabernacle. He didn't even know how to drive a nail. He was a shepherd, not a carpenter. So God told Moses to find these two men, Bezalel and Oholiab, and to hand the project over to them. The Lord explained to Moses that he had specially prepared Bezalel and Oholiab for this work. Throughout their lives, they had learned everything they would need to know about carpentry, sewing, and metallurgy so they could lead the way in building this house for the Lord. But not only could these two men do everything that was necessary in order to construct the tabernacle according to God's specific blueprint; they also had the ability to organize, teach, and manage others who would assist them in this great work. So God gave the vision to Moses, but he gave the talent to Bezalel and Oholiab.

Then God instructed Moses to take an offering from the people (the first offering in the Bible). God told Moses that he wanted the people to contribute all the wood, precious metals, fragrances, oils, and fabrics that would be used to construct the tabernacle. This means that Moses had the vision, Bezalel and Oholiab had the talent, and the people had the means. So every person did what he could do, and the project moved forward. Every person offered his own unique contribution to the Lord, and the vision was realized. But nobody would have been successful and the project would not have been completed unless every person did his part. This means that nobody except God could take the credit when the project was finished, but everybody could share in the joy of achieving God's purpose. So nobody would be conceited about the success of the project and nobody would feel left out. Nobody would suffer from pride and nobody would suffer from low self-esteem.

Notice, however, that Moses didn't try to drive nails, and the people didn't try to overlay handmade woodcarvings with liquid gold. Every person offered his strengths to the Lord, but every person respected his boundaries. Likewise, you are a unique individual. God made you to be different from every other person in the world. Nobody has your unique fingerprint. Nobody has your unique retinal scan. Nobody has your DNA coding. You are truly one of a kind, and you have a one-of-a-kind destiny and a one-of-a-kind blend of talents. You should appreciate and embrace your uniqueness, but you also should accept your limitations, because, while the person beside you can't cook like you or bring a smile to the face of a hurting child like you can, you can't add numbers in your head like her or recite poetry from memory like him. And while she may be thinner, you may be smarter.

When you start seeing yourself differently, when you start appreciating your strengths and respecting your limitations, when you start embracing the special qualities that God has given to you and stop envying the ones he gave to others, you will start seeing everyone else differently, too, and they will see you differently, because your perceptions shape your reality, and a changed perspective can actually change your world. It can certainly change you. So take some time to look at yourself in the mirror, and ask yourself honestly what you see. Do you see something you like or something you dislike? Are you encouraged by what you see or discouraged? Be honest with yourself, but be fair.

For years, whenever I looked in the mirror on the wall, I saw damaged goods. I saw a skinny, brown-haired, blue-eyed girl who was barely surviving and immensely unsure of herself. I saw a defeated, miserable girl who was worthy of nothing good, a girl who was unlovable, because she didn't know how to love herself or others. When I looked in the mirror, I saw a girl in search of herself, a young, foolish girl who was on a journey to nowhere. As life seemingly moved forward for others, she failed to make any progress. Instead, she only found more areas of concern and more things to hate about herself and her own developing body. I saw a girl that nobody wanted and who everyone despised, a girl who was neither an "A" student nor a cheerleader nor a homecoming queen. Instead, all I saw was defeat and a pathetic character who was worthy of the low self-esteem she exhibited.

From my early teenage years, I battled with such intense self-esteem issues that I actually put bruises on my own body. I would stare in the mirror and then literally beat myself up. That's right! I would hit myself until I produced visible wounds, and I would pull my hair until it came out in my hands. And when I wasn't looking in the mirror, I would talk negatively to myself—sometimes out loud—telling myself how pathetic I was and how useless. I was a terribly unhealthy young woman on a desperate search for importance. I needed the Lord to transform me and to pull me out of the terrible pit I had fallen into.

But I was looking in all the wrong places for his help. I was looking "outward" toward others, thinking God should make me like them so I could be happy and popular. But what I really needed was to realize the vanity and insanity of comparing myself with other flawed human beings (their flaws are always carefully concealed). And instead, I needed to see my own value and self worth as a special creation of God. I needed to see how much Jesus loved me and how valuable I was to him, so his love could transform the opinion I held of myself.

Then one day, my eyes were opened and I saw myself in a whole new light. For the first time, I saw myself the way that God sees me. The person God made me to be was always there, right in front of my eyes. She was staring back at me every time I gazed into the mirror. But when your thinking is distorted and your mind is focused on everything that is negative, your eyes cannot see the beauty and the potential that is right in front of you. Perhaps this is what Isaiah, Jeremiah, Ezekiel, and Jesus meant when they spoke about having eyes, but not being able to see (compare Isaiah 6:10, Jeremiah 5:21, Ezekiel 12:2, and Mark 8:18). In fact, when I read my Bible, it is amazing to me how many people were unable to fulfill their God-given destinies because they were not able to see what God saw when he looked at them and the circumstances that confronted them.

In Luke 10, for instance, Jesus told a story about a man who was attacked and beaten on his way from Jerusalem to Jericho. A priest and a Levite passed this injured man without helping him. But then a Samaritan passed by. According to Jesus, *"When (the Samaritan) saw him, he took pity on (the injured man)"* (Luke 10:33). The injured man was there all the time, but until the Samaritan "saw him," he didn't do anything to change the man's plight. Until the Samaritan's eyes were opened to see the man's need and his own ability to do something about that need, he did not reach out to help the man. Too often in life, things are already true and things are already real, but we just can't see them. Our eyes are closed or our eyes are focused on other things so that we cannot see the obvious, and we look beyond or through the person or the situation that is right in front of us without even noticing it, without really even seeing it.

On another occasion, Jesus traveled across the Sea of Galilee to the region of the Gerasenes. When he got out of the boat, a man with an unclean spirit came out from among the tombs and approached him. Describing the actions of the demon-possessed man, the biblical account explains that *"when he saw Jesus from a distance, he ran and fell on his knees in front of him"* (Mark 5:6). Jesus had been there all the time, ministering in the cities and small towns around the Sea of Galilee. But when he came close to the man in the tombs and when this man finally laid his eyes on Jesus for the very first time, the vile spirit within the man was forced to respond. We typically respond to what we see.

The truths of God's Word are objectively true before we even notice them. They were true when they were written, they were true before you were born, and they are true today. But if you can't "see" them, they won't work in your life. It's a little like having a million dollars in the bank when you don't know that it's there.

Imagine how you would feel if you learned that 30 years ago a distant relative had left you $1 million in his will and that the executor of the estate had deposited your million dollars in a local bank in your name. But you never got the letter, informing you that the money had been bequeathed to you. Finally, after 30 years had passed, an officer at the bank decided to contact you to let you know that the account had grown exponentially due to the compound interest that had accumulated over those 30 years. And now you had an amazing sum of money in a bank just two blocks from your house. How would you feel about such news?

Obviously, you would be happy to be so blessed. But you also would be angry. Think of all the things you could have done with that money over the past 30 years. Think of the way that large sum of money could have improved your life and the lives of your family members. You could have worked less and spent more time with your children while they were young. You could have helped your husband build that business he always dreamed about. You could have helped your aging parents when your dad got sick and they had to sell their house.

That's exactly the way it is when our eyes are shut. When we can't see the truth when the truth is right in front of us, the truth won't do us any good. Like a person with a hidden bank account, the man who cannot see the wealth of his own life is a man who is living in poverty. He is living beneath his potential and his means. But when our eyes are finally opened and we are able to see the truth, there is immediate freedom. There also is an immediate sense of gratitude and personal value.

When I saw, for the very first time, a girl who had a friend in Jesus, I found my significance. I found my own worth. I found my life's potential. I found my strength and the necessary confidence to do anything and everything that fell within the venue of my created potential. I no longer focused on the things I wasn't. Instead, I focused on the things I was, and I left it to others to be those things that I wasn't designed to be. And that simple change of focus changed my life and my destiny in a way that forever altered the course of my life.

But once again, I didn't get to the Promised Land overnight (the theme of this book in case you haven't noticed by now). The epiphany that enabled me to see the truth and to wake up to reality was the spark plug that ignited the engine of my soul to make some necessary changes. It was definitely a turning point and a watershed moment in my life. But walking out the things that I "saw" when I gazed into my mirror on that momentous day took weeks, months, and years. And I am still learning to walk out the truth that was made real to me that day, the truth that I am a unique creation, that I have a God-given purpose which nobody else can fulfill, and that I have incalculable worth and unlimited potential to be everything God made me to be, but not something he did not make me to be.

Many times since then I have been willing to change, but I didn't know how to change. I didn't know what to do. So I followed the tried-and-true formula that has worked for me in every other area of my life. I seized the momentum created by a moment of revelation and then I moved forward by taking baby steps, patiently granting myself the necessary time I would need to make my predictable mistakes and to learn from them as I figured out how to make use of this new knowledge.

One of the first "baby steps" for me was to look in the mirror regularly and compliment myself. That's right! I would actually gaze into my own eyes and tell myself what I appreciated about myself. I would talk about the good things that I was seeing. But I also would take an honest look at the things I didn't like about myself, and I would ask myself some difficult, but constructive questions so I could confront my own tendency to constantly put myself down.

I would ask myself, "What is it I don't like about what I see?" Then I would ask, "Why?" But after that, I would ask myself some healthy questions about these unappealing qualities, questions I had never asked in the past. I would ask myself: "Did God create me this way, or is this particular trait something I have the ability to change?" And finally, I would ask myself the kinds of questions that would lead to a wholesome way of thinking about myself: "If this is the way I was created to be, how can I change my attitude about this trait and learn to accept it and to glorify the Lord through it? But if this is not the way I was created to be, what can I do to stop feeling sorry for myself and to change that personal quality which is bringing me so much displeasure?"

By doing things like this on a daily basis, I finally began to realize that I had potential, value, worth, and purpose. I finally began to like myself, and I realized that my strengths and weaknesses were pretty well balanced. I realized that my strengths were directly attached to my destiny and that I was responsible to God for developing them. But I also realized that my weaknesses were given to me to keep me humble and to keep me dependent on God and appreciative of others who could do what I could not do. Over time, therefore, I learned to embrace those things that were part of me and to take deliberate steps to change those things about myself that were acquired rather than created. This approach to "self" has made all the difference in my life.

So when I visited the mirror each day, I would tell myself that I liked myself, and eventually that confession began to sink in and I really started believing it. I also told myself that I believed in myself and in my ability to change those things about myself that were not part of God's plan when he originally designed me. A person will eventually believe what he or she continuously hears, so I made sure I heard these things every day from my own lips. The truth makes a big difference.

By faith, I came to realize that God created this "cute" package and that everything he created was good. I also came to realize that God had given me the power to change almost anything about myself that wasn't part of his original blueprint for me. So for months, I would regularly visit my mirror and proclaim positive confessions over my own life. Then, once those confessions began to impact my thinking and once they began to affect the way I felt about myself, I began to journal the things that I was thinking about "me." I also began to write little post-it notes to myself and stick them everywhere, reaffirming the things I had been telling myself in front of the mirror. Hey! Whatever works, works! And, of course, I read my Bible regularly, paying close attention to all the things God was saying to me about myself and how he viewed me, and I posted those scriptures on my mirror so I could read them and confess them every day as I visited with myself.

Before I knew it, my mind was rejuvenated. My heart felt happy again, and my spirit was lifted. In time, I was able to see that I was created in God's image, and I finally saw in myself what God saw in me: a young woman he loved very much, a special young lady who had gifts and talents and attributes in a combination that nobody else possessed, a girl who had great potential and whose heart was a dwelling place for the Lord. I also saw my responsibility toward God as I came to realize how he wanted me to use my special attributes to serve him by serving others. So I saw purpose, and I saw significance.

But I also saw my own limitations, which I finally understood. I saw that I could do almost anything I wanted to do, but that I could not do everything. I could be almost anything I wanted to be, but I could not be everything. I was dependent on God for those things that only he could do in my life. And I was dependent on others for those special qualities God had placed within them so they could serve me in my areas of need. I was finally beginning to see myself, others, life, and God in an accurate way. I was finally beginning to love myself and to enjoy my life without becoming depressed or envious.

Yes, I stumble occasionally, as I do with my personal organization and with the other disciplines of life that I have mentioned in this book. I am not perfect, and I will never be perfect. I continue to struggle sometimes with people and with their defeating words, which occasionally affect my heart in a deep way despite all my efforts to resist them. But now, when this occurs, I go straight to the Word of God to find out what the Lord has to say about me. And when God's assessment of me conflicts with someone else's assessment, I accept God's appraisal and I confess it to myself until it eventually overwhelms the dark lies that were spoken to inflict pain and spiritual death.

I also make sure that I surround myself with positive people who truly care about me and have my best interests at heart, people who encourage me and build me up with their words. And I make sure to regularly encourage myself by telling myself that I love myself in the same way that God loves me. I tell myself how proud I am of myself in the same way that God is proud of me.

Like I said, this is a process, not an event. It is slow and it is sometimes painful and agonizing, but it will be well worth the effort and it will produce life-changing results if you can begin to see yourself in a more wholesome and balanced way. When you finally let your heart focus on the truths of God's Word and when you begin to teach your mouth to say the same things about God, about others, about life, and about yourself that God is saying, your world will be turned upside down and your spirit will be edified and elevated. You will be changed as a person, and the course of your life will be altered forever.

So I challenge you to start looking in the mirror in a brand new way. At first, learn to like a few things about yourself, and then learn to actually love what you see. But the key is to be honest with yourself and to let God take that tiny ember of willingness that you have presented to him and turn it into a spreading flame of passion for growth and change. It also would be helpful if you made daily confessions to yourself, confessions that can fortify within you those things that are biblically and objectively true. For example:

- God sees me as a strong and courageous person.
- God sees me as an intelligent person.
- I am created in the image and likeness of God.
- God sees me as a person filled with potential.
- God knows the real me, and he loves the real me.
- I am blessed, and I am on my way to victory.

But don't stop there. Couple your own positive confessions with the confessions of God's Word and watch what happens in your life. Resist the negative appraisals the world would make of you and watch the devil flee from you (see James 4:7). Appreciate the greatness that God designed within you and watch that greatness emerge and take shape before your very eyes.

Perhaps you can start with the words of some of the psalmists, who apparently fought a similar emotional battle with negative thoughts and feelings. Let their inspired words strengthen you as those words have strengthened me, and let them uplift you as you seek to view yourself from God's perspective rather than the negative perspective instilled in you by others.

Remember the words of the writer of the 94th Psalm, who wrote, "When doubts filled my mind, your comfort gave me renewed hope and cheer" (Psalm 94:19, NLT). And remember the words of the longest psalm in the Bible, which reminds us, "Abundant peace belongs to those who love Your instruction; nothing makes them stumble" (Psalm 119:165, Holman).

Formidable weapons are aimed at us every day in an effort to defeat us and to neutralize the plan of God for our lives. But God has given us more effective weapons to use in our defense as we strive to overcome the negative thoughts of the world and to conquer the negative things we repeat to ourselves. The Lord has not left us helpless in our search for significance. He has given us effective ways to appropriate his truths in our hearts and his peace in our lives. So continue to feed your mind with truth, and allow your spirit to soar to new heights as you gaze into the mirror at someone God deeply loves.

MODULE 6

MIRROR, MIRROR ON THE WALL

MIRROR, MIRROR ON THE WALL

1. Pride and arrogance, egotism and haughtiness, are the root cause of every sin and every spiritual malady. When you take an honest look at yourself, do you see a prideful person? In what ways?

_____

_____

_____

2. Do you tend to think too highly of yourself? Too lowly? What attitudes and behaviors point to this tendency in your life?

_____

_____

_____

3. What are the genuine strengths that God has placed within you? What are the limitations that annoy you?

_____

_____

_____

4. Drawing from Paul's analogy of the human body in I Corinthians 12, where he compares the members of the church to the various "members" of the human body, what part of the human body do you believe best describes your assigned role in the work of God and in life? Why?

_____

_____

_____

5. Do you tend to suffer from envy? What do you envy about other people? How does envy express itself in your life?

_____

_____

_____

6. Christine Martin explains that there was a time when she "no longer focused on the things I wasn't. Instead, I focused on the things I was, and I left it to others to be those things that I wasn't designed to be." What things fall into the "wasn't" category for you? What things do you sometimes try to be that you were not created to be?

_____

_____

7. You have unlimited potential to be everything God made you to be, but not something he did not make you to be. So what did God make you to be? And if you aren't sure, how can you learn the answer to this question?

8. Right now, when you look into the mirror on the wall, what is it you don't like about what you see? Why?

9. Do the negative and hurtful words of others tend to affect you deeply or only slightly? How do you deal with such words?

10. Christine Martin regularly confesses to herself that "God knows the real me, and he loves the real me." Do you believe that God knows and loves you just the way you are? Why?

_____

_____

DIGGING DEEPER

According to Christine Martin, people tend to view themselves in one of three ways. People can view themselves as other people see them, they can view themselves through their own eyes, or they can view themselves as God sees them.

Do you tend to view yourself as other people see you? In your opinion, what causes a person to view himself this way? What can someone do to overcome this tendency?

_____

_____

_____

Do you tend to view yourself through your own eyes? Does this give you an accurate appraisal of yourself? Why or why not?

_____

_____

_____

Do you tend to view yourself from God's perspective? What is God's perspective of you? How does God's perspective differ from the perspective of others and yourself?

_____

_____

_____

WHEN YOUR EYES ARE OPENED

But a Samaritan, as he traveled, came where the man was; and when he saw him, he took pity on him. He went to him and bandaged his wounds, pouring on oil and wine. Then he put the man on his own donkey, brought him to an inn and took care of him.
Luke 10:33-34

Every human being knows what it is like to have his perceptions changed. Most of the time, a change in perception flows from a deep personal experience that causes a person to see something old in a completely new way. But whether it's a traumatic experience or an encounter with God or a slow process of change that brings us to the place where we look at familiar things in a different way, the truth remains that no person can really change his behavior until he changes his perceptions.

Perhaps the recent death of a grandparent has caused you to see old age in a new way, or perhaps the promotion of one of your colleagues at work has caused you to see hard work in a new way. Maybe the birth of your first child has caused you to see your role in life in a new way, or maybe a recent traffic accident has caused you to see the responsibility of driving in a new way.

As humans, we tend to look right through and beyond the things that are in front of us until something happens to reshape the way we view those things. We are so busy getting to where we are going, we fail to notice the other drivers or the scenery or the road signs we never read. But when something happens that makes us take the time to look and we couple our observations with serious thought, the things we see can change right before our eyes.

The Samaritan saw the wounded man, and he took action to change the man's circumstances. But until he "saw" this wounded man, the Samaritan did nothing. With our eyes we see, but then our eyes compel us to take action to engage the things we actually observe.

SOMETHING TO THINK ABOUT

According to the implicit teachings of God's Word, people tend to fall into three distinct categories when it comes to the appraisal they hold of themselves. Like the three bears in the famous fairy tale, some think of themselves too highly (too hot), some think of themselves too lowly (too cold), and some think of themselves appropriately and with balance (just right).

How can you recognize the difference between the person who is confident in his "anointing" and the person who is cocky or arrogant? Do you see any of these same tendencies in your own life?

_____

_____

_____

Do any of the people closest to you tend to think of themselves too lowly? How can you tell? How do their attitudes toward themselves impact you and make you feel?

_____

_____

_____

Do you know someone (other than yourself) who seems to have an accurate and balanced appraisal of himself? How do you feel about this person? Does his (or her) demeanor and self-esteem elevate your appraisal of him or weaken him in your eyes?

_____

_____

_____

MY PRAYER FOR PERCEPTION

Father, help me see things the way you see them. I know that you rebuked the prophet Samuel when he was impressed by Eliab, David's older brother. You told him that *"man looks at the outward appearance, but the LORD looks at the heart"* (I Samuel 16:7, NIV). And then you instructed Samuel to anoint David to be the next king of Israel, even though David was much younger and much less impressive than his big brother. Help me not to fall into that same trap, Lord. Help me to see all things and all people through your eyes. Especially help me to see myself the way that you see me. If I can see myself properly, then I know that my vision will be trustworthy whenever I look elsewhere. I want to see myself, my life, and my place in your kingdom the way that you see them. In Jesus' name, Amen!

MY SPIRITUAL JOURNAL

Take a few moments to record your thoughts regarding this week's session on perception and self-image. What new things did you learn? What new insights and revelations have you had? What life-changing truths did Christine Martin impart that have impacted your thinking? What changes will you make in the days ahead?

_____

_____

_____

FOOD FOR THOUGHT

The Bible describes God's Words as spiritual bread and spiritual meat. It is designed to nourish the spirit and the soul in the same way that food nourishes the body. So read the following scripture every day this week, repeating it out loud when you read it, and memorize it, if possible. And while you meditate upon this passage, make notes about anything you may observe about your personal life and any changes you may want to make.

*Then I heard the voice of the Lord saying, "Whom shall I
send? And who will go for us?" And I said, "Here am I. Send
me!" He said, "Go and tell this people: 'Be ever hearing, but
never understanding; be ever seeing, but never perceiving.
Make the heart of this people calloused; make their ears dull
and close their eyes. Otherwise they might see with their eyes,
hear with their ears, understand with their hearts, and turn
and be healed.'"* Isaiah 6:8-10

WISDOM FROM ABOVE

*When doubts filled my mind, your comfort gave me
renewed hope and cheer.*
Psalm 94:19 (NLT)

*Pride goes before destruction, a haughty spirit before a
fall.*
Proverbs 16:18

*For by the grace given me I say to every one of you: Do
not think of yourself more highly than you ought, but rather
think of yourself with sober judgment, in accordance with
the faith God has distributed to each of you.*
Romans 12:3

COULD YOU REPEAT THAT?

The way you see yourself makes a world of difference in the way you live your life and the way you feel about yourself.

God doesn't want us to think of ourselves too highly (too hot) or too lowly (too cold). Instead, God wants us to think of ourselves "just right."

When we can't see the truth when the truth is right in front of us, the truth won't do us any good.

IN A NUTSHELL

I have incalculable worth and unlimited potential to be everything God made me to be, but not something he did not make me to be.

CHAPTER 7

Seasons Change

If you've been around long enough to remember the 60s, then you recall a very popular song recorded during that time by The Byrds. The song Turn! Turn! Turn! was actually written by Pete Seeger six years before The Byrds recorded it, and it remains one of the most popular classics of that era. But what you may not know is that the lyrics of the song were taken completely from the book of Ecclesiastes (with the exception of the last line). Those who are familiar with the song are impressed by the beauty and the flow of the biblical text.

Solomon wrote, *"To every thing there is a season, and a time to every purpose under heaven: a time to be born, and a time to die; a time to plant, and a time to pluck up that which is planted; a time to kill, and a time to heal; a time to break down, and a time to build up; a time to weep, and a time to laugh; a time to mourn, and a time to dance; a time to cast away stones, and a time to gather stones together; a time to embrace, and a time to refrain from embracing; a time to get, and a time to lose; a time to keep, and a time to cast away; a*

time to rend, and a time to sew; a time to keep silence, and a
time to speak; a time to love, and a time to hate; a time of war,
and a time of peace" (Ecclesiastes 3:1-8, KJV).

There are multiple spiritual truths to be gleaned from
this memorable excerpt from the writings of Solomon. But
the truth I want to extract and analyze in this chapter is the
truth that no condition is permanent. Life is like the ebb and
flow of the ocean tides; it constantly changes. In fact, one of
the most accurate comparisons we could summon to help us
understand the changing nature of life is the changing nature
of God's creation. The world that God made never stands
still. It changes slowly, but it changes constantly and it usually changes predictably.

In life, as in nature, there are seasons, and these seasons
come and go. They change. Some people don't like the changing seasons. They would prefer the temperature and foliage
to remain constant throughout the year. But the vast majority
of people appreciate the changing seasons. In fact, where I
live, in Florida, I see vivid evidence of this every day. During the winter months, when the temperatures in Florida are
moderate and pleasant, northerners migrate here by the mil-
lions (we call them "snow birds"). But Floridians, who get
tired of swimming twelve months out of the year, pack up
their gear and head to North Carolina or Colorado to go ski-
ing. Most people appreciate the refreshing nature of change.

But the lesson we can glean from Solomon's observations and from the changing nature of God's creation is that nothing remains forever in its present state (except God himself). Everything is destined to change. And this is good news, because this means that none of life's trials will last either. They must eventually change, as well.

You may be familiar with the old adage, "This too shall pass." The origins of this phrase are uncertain, but the saying appears to date back to ancient Persia. And sometimes Solomon has been credited with the authorship of this expression. The adage apparently originated as part of a fable about a powerful king who assigned his wise men and counselors the responsibility of making a ring for him that would help him remain emotionally balanced under any circumstances. He wanted a ring that would lift his spirit when he felt sad and humble him when he felt empowered. After much thought, the king's advisors designed a ring for him with the inscription, "This too shall pass." The king was pleased.

Even though this phrase is not in the Bible, the same sentiment is communicated through the book of Ecclesiastes. God wants us to know that things change. Nothing remains the same. Tribulations are temporary, but so are the specific joys of life. Even our relationships are destined to change and ultimately destined to end. The only thing that is eternal in our lives is our ongoing relationship with God.

This is sobering news, because it means that we must extract all the delight that we can possibly squeeze out of the precious moments of life, because those moments are fleeting. But this also is welcome news, because it means that it is possible to be happy in the midst of the storm. It means that the storm will eventually blow over and the clouds will dissipate. So the message here for the believer is that he should be happy in life, even when things are going badly, because his circumstances will surely change. Change, therefore, is inevitable, but misery is optional, because misery refuses to accept the changing nature of life.

I know the importance of planning. In fact, I wrote an entire chapter in this book to deal with the issues of organization and planning. If you fail to plan, you plan to fail. At the same time, however, I believe in balance. In fact, I believe that balance is more important than almost anything in life. Without balance, it is possible to be too organized. It is possible to plan so much that you actually fail to live the life you are planning.

Some people believe in one-year plans for their lives. Other people believe in five-year plans or ten-year plans. And still others have plans that extend farther into the future. The Japanese are known for writing 100-year goals for their lives. So I understand that you have to plan some things, because certain things in life are inevitable. My son will probably want to go to college one day, and Dave and I will probably want to retire when we finally reach our late 20s (just kidding). So I understand that it is unwise to throw caution to the wind and live life without any forethought whatsoever.

But come on! Life is not that predictable. Things change, so our plans need to be flexible enough to accommodate those inevitable changes.

I can put money back to plan for my son's college education, but college might not be a viable option for him once he figures out what he wants to do with his life. Dave and I can piece together a retirement plan, but changes in the tax code and entitlement reforms might make our plans obsolete before we can fulfill them. So I am careful not to plan too much or too far ahead. I am careful to leave some things to providence and some things to spontaneity. God will help me modify my course as long as I don't get completely careless and unconcerned about tomorrow's consequences for today's choices.

But why do I have this "loosey-goosey" attitude toward long-term planning? Because things change! Seasons change. So my plans have to change with them if I intend to stay current and engaged. To have a plan, any plan, that is totally inflexible and void of adaptability is to hem oneself into the way that things are right now and to neglect the fact that things are destined to change.

Once again, let me resort to nature to illustrate my point. Here in Florida, we have a lot of palm trees. In fact, we have several varieties of palm trees, and they can be found everywhere. But there are two reasons that palm trees thrive in the subtropical environment of Central Florida. First, they are definitely warm-weather plants. They cannot survive in places that are cold. But just as important, palm trees are resilient. They are flexible. When the winds blow really hard (and Florida is famous for hurricanes), a palm tree can bend all the way over and touch the ground without breaking or uprooting. And then it snaps back into its upright position once the winds cease. Perhaps that is why the psalmist wrote, *"The righteous will flourish like a palm tree"* (Psalm 92:12).

God's people need to be like the palm tree. We need to bend a little. We need to stretch a little. We need to be flexible and not so stiff. We need to ride out the storms of life instead of breaking ourselves by trying to resist them. Sometimes, we just need to be patient and wait for the storm to pass and for the sun to come out again.

If you want to succeed in life, you must be prepared to change. If you can discover how to successfully deal with change, you will enjoy your life much more and you will be much more productive. You also will experience less stress and more success in your work and your personal life. Your spirit will be lifted as you face the reality of change with the right kind of attitude and the right type of response.

Many people become disheartened and discouraged because of life's changing nature. Some people just can't handle change. They don't like it, and they resist it. So the constant, ongoing struggle between the way life is and the way they want life to be creates sadness within their souls. But the facts of life are that change is inevitable, that change is ceaseless, and that change is both good and bad in nature. It is good in the sense that the unpleasant parts of life eventually pass us by, but it is bad in the sense that the enjoyable parts of life change too. Fortunately, new pleasures come with new seasons. Nevertheless, while some people can see the positive aspects of change, others cannot. Instead, these people are distraught because they cannot believe that the storms will ever blow over and they cannot understand that the joyous aspects of life are destined to be replaced by new and exciting experiences.

The most reliable pathway to discouragement is the pathway that is paved with unrealistic expectations. If you are intent on embracing unrealistic expectations of life, you are setting yourself up for certain disappointment and defeat. Therefore, to help you avoid becoming discouraged by adopting naive expectancies, let me point you to a few truthful and necessary things you need to know about the changing nature of life in this world. If you can understand change and how God wants you to deal with it, change can actually become a positive force in your life instead of a source of sorrow.

First, change happens.

Earlier in this chapter, I told you that, if you want to succeed in life, you must be prepared to change. But I also need to tell you that, if you want to succeed in life, you must be prepared for change.

Change is inevitable, and change is endless. In fact, the only thing in this world that never changes is change itself. Whether you like change or not, change is a force you cannot control. It will happen every year, every month, every week, and every day of your life. The minute you get comfortable with something, it will change. Change is as predictable as the sunrise. Nothing remains the same forever.

How long have you been alive? In the few short years of my life, I have seen changes that are almost impossible to believe. I have friends who are older than me who have seen changes that are even more profound than the ones I have witnessed. For instance, I have a friend who is helping me get this book ready for publication, and he told me how he traveled to Cape Canaveral when he was a child to watch the launch of Apollo 11, the first manned spaceflight to the moon. My friend also told me about his grandfather, who was born before the Wright Brothers flew their first airplane and who sat in front of his own television set to watch Neil Armstrong take the first step on the surface of the moon. The changes that have taken place in recent years are beyond comprehension.

But the pace of change is actually accelerating. Things have always changed, but not at the pace they are changing right now. In politics, in technology, in communication, in entertainment, and even in family and social dynamics, the world looks completely different than it did just a generation ago. While our parents were proud to have an 8-track player mounted beneath the dashboard of their car, we walk around with miniature iPods that can hold thousands of recorded songs and with even smaller cell phones that can instantly access any song ever recorded by any artist who ever lived in any country that ever existed at any time that ever was. And who knows what tomorrow's technology will do?

But technology is just the tip of the iceberg. The greatest changes I have observed in my lifetime are the social and political changes. People think differently. They relate to one another differently. They expect different things from their government and their employers. Commerce is different. The Internet has revolutionized everything in our lives. And social media has completely revamped the way we relate to one another and even the way we meet one another and fall in love.

If you don't like change, you might want to relocate to a different planet, because change is the one undeniable and predictable force of life that is never going to go away. In fact, it is only going to intensify. And it is going to intensify at an ever-increasing pace. The way you pay your bills today, the way you communicate with your friends today, the car you drive, the food you eat, the clothes you wear, and even the way your church worships God will all change before you depart this world. So get used to it. Accept it. And learn to live with change instead of allowing change to stress you out and pull you down. Have fun with it.

Change is not a bad thing. Change is not always a good thing either. As I have explained, change is both positive and negative. While every change brings greater convenience, lower cost, or faster access, every change also takes away something with which we are familiar and creates another challenge in our lives. Accept change as real, therefore, and accept it as inevitable. Learn to cope with it, handle it, and even employ it to your benefit. But also learn to respect it and to understand its inherent difficulties.

If you do not learn to accept change as inevitable and to embrace change as a positive force, you will become extinct like the dinosaurs or obsolete like the village blacksmith. So get with it and get current. Go with the flow and make the best of those changes that happen all around you.

Second, anticipate change.

If this many changes have occurred in your short lifetime and mine, just imagine how many more changes we can expect in the days to come. As they say, "You ain't seen nothin' yet!" Personally, I can't imagine what changes might occur in the future, and that's what makes the future so exciting and a little bit frightening at the same time.

If the black-and-white movies that my parents watched are now being replaced with 3-D animation and sound effects that can actually shake the theater, just imagine what kind of movies we will be watching ten years from now or twenty. If I can pull out my cell phone while my husband and I are driving through Orlando, Florida, and take an online "virtual tour" of a condo we are thinking about renting in Alberta, Canada, just imagine what my son will be able to do with a telephone when he is my age.

Starting right now, adopt a mindset that anticipates change, recognizes change when it is happening, and embraces the positive aspects of change. Be ready, both mentally and practically, to move on when society takes its next step forward. You don't necessarily have to like every change that takes place around you, but you do have to participate in it. Whether you like it or not, you are like a cork floating in a rushing stream. The fast current of change is taking you places you may not want to go, but you don't possess the wherewithal to swim against the tide or the means to plot a different course. So you might as well enjoy the ride and participate in life while you are traveling through it. To resist the currents of change is to wear yourself out in a losing cause and to miss all the benefits you might otherwise derive from the positive advances of society.

In fact, the rushing stream is swelling. The rains keep coming, so the pace of the current is picking up and the waters are rising and overflowing their banks. You are going to get swept up in the current and swallowed by the floodwaters, whether you like it or not. So you can either put on your bathing suit and have fun, or you can buy a life jacket and kill yourself trying to swim against the tide.

But while you will invariably exhaust and isolate yourself by resisting the currents of change, the tide of change will only grow stronger. The good news, however, is that this is designed to work in your favor. As I have explained, the changing nature of life means that the bad elements of your life will change, too. Your trials will serve their purpose and expire. Your conflicts will resolve themselves in due season. Your problems will find a solution. Your troubles will dissipate and become a distant memory.

So don't give up. Expect things to change, because things will change. A crisis is always found at the curve of a change, so the crisis you are facing today will soon be behind you as you work your way around the curve and enter a new stretch of the highway to your future. As the song says, "The sun will come out tomorrow." So don't allow the joys and blessings of this day to be wasted because you have convinced yourself that every day will be like this one.

You will never again be where you are today. And even though that might sound really nice if you are currently facing a difficult trial, the fact remains that you also may lose the good things you enjoy today when tomorrow finally arrives. For one thing, your children won't ever be this age again. For another thing, you and your husband (or wife) won't ever be at this place in your life again. You may never again do the things you do today or share experiences with the people you share them with today. So don't let today's problems rob you of today's happiness, because, while today's problems are destined to end, so are today's pleasures. And while tomorrow will bring a brand new set of joys, it also will present you with a brand new set of difficulties. So learn to anticipate change and to be ready for it. And learn to live life to the fullest today as you look forward to those things that tomorrow will bring your way.

Third, monitor change.

Know what is happening around you. Be relevant. Don't curse the rising tides of change. Instead, be aware of change and participate in it.

Are you old? Obviously, your first response to a question like this would be, "How old is 'old'? Is 40 'old'? Is 70 'old'?" If you're like me, you believe that "old" is a relative term. In my way of thinking, a person is "old" when that person can no longer change. When a person starts believing that all the best things are behind him and that he must stubbornly cling to the past if he wants to be happy, that person has crossed the line. He is no longer "young"; instead he is "old."

Just think about it! When you were young, you were always excited about the newest song or the newest movie. You were always fascinated by the newest fashions and the newest gadgets at the store. But as you grew older, you became

RECHARGED

less interested in those things. You didn't want to constantly trade your old devices for new ones. You didn't want to constantly look for new television programs to watch in place of the ones you had come to enjoy. It's understandable that you would become comfortable with certain things and familiar with certain processes. But if you're not careful, you can allow yourself to become totally resistant to change. And that makes you "old" and irrelevant.

You're "old" when you can no longer adapt to your environment. You're "old" when you can no longer "bend" in order to accommodate the winds of change. When you start standing stubbornly in defiance of change, you are no longer like the palm tree, which is designed to withstand the storms of life by submitting to them. Instead, you become like a manufactured house, inflexible and fragile. And the winds are going to break you.

So know what is happening around you and why. This doesn't mean that you have to give your approval to all the changes that take place in the world. But it does mean that you are cognizant of them so you can accept those changes that are beneficial to you and respond with wisdom to those that are not.

Fourth, adapt to change quickly.

Steve Jobs, who died in 2011, was one of the most successful and respected CEOs in American history. He was renowned for founding and managing Apple, Inc. But the thing that made Jobs so successful was the fact that he could sense the winds of change in American culture perhaps better than anyone. He accumulated billions of dollars and made tens of thousands of people wealthy because he had an uncanny knack for sensing where the culture was heading and staying one step ahead of them by creating the gadgets they would need to get there.

The faster you let go of the past, the faster you can enjoy the future, because the past and the future are a little like Elsa in Indiana Jones and the Last Crusade. If you recall, Elsa fell to her death in an abyss because she would not give her free hand to Indiana. While dangling by one hand, she desperately tried to reach the Holy Grail with the other hand, and she died as a result. If she had let go of the Grail and had given her free hand to Indiana, he would have pulled her out of the abyss and she would have survived.

So if you want to survive to embrace the future, you have to release the past. If you want to live in the future, you have to leave the past behind. This doesn't mean that you can't relish your past memories or continue enjoying some of the things you enjoyed when you were younger. The best things in life endure for a lifetime. But when you just can't enjoy anything that is different or new because you are trapped in the things that are comfortable and old, you are not growing; you are dying.

The quicker you let go of what worked yesterday, the sooner you can enjoy the benefits of what is working today. The faster you let go of what worked well, the sooner you can enjoy the benefits of what is working better. So try to start noticing changes and trends early on, either to take advantage of them or to brace yourself for the tsunami of change that is coming, because change is coming and it is coming with more turbulence than ever.

Fifth, learn how to change.

Move! Shift positions! Change your hair, rearrange your furniture, or try something different for dinner. But please, do something! Don't just sit there and waste away while clinging to the past. Participate in today, and anticipate tomorrow.

I love Christians. I am a Christian myself, and I would rather be around God's people than any other people in the world. But Christians are notorious for resisting change. They like to sing the same old songs, week after week. They like to sit in the same old spot on the pew, month and after month. And they like to do the same old things in their churches, year after year. Homecoming! The spring revival! The ladies' auxiliary meeting!

There's nothing wrong with traditions. In fact, the people of God in the Bible had a lot of rich traditions that carried a great deal of meaning and met real spiritual needs. But come on! You can live in the past so staunchly that you totally miss today and tomorrow, and that was one of the biggest problems the Jews had throughout their history. They always blew the past up so big in their minds that it became a legend that transcended reality. But they always missed what God was doing right in front of them, and they had very little understanding of the future.

God wants us to remember the past and to draw from it (see I Corinthians 10:11). But God also wants to do something new in our lives. In the Bible, we learn that believers will sing a new song (Revelation 5:9; 14:3), that God wants every person to experience the new birth (see John 3:6-7), that each of God's children will receive a new name (see Revelation 2:17), and that the Lord will get rid of this world and create a new heaven and new earth (see II Peter 3:13; Revelation 21:1). The Bible also mentions new wine, a new heart, and a new thing. It mentions a new spirit, a new covenant, and a new day.

"All things are become new," the Lord told the apostle Paul (II Corinthians 5:17, KJV). So why do God's people persist in clinging to the old ways? We cling to the past because of memories. We cling to the past because of powerful and precious experiences. Then we associate those experiences with God. If we came to learn about God at a youth camp where services were held at night under a tent with sawdust on the ground, we will always equate the presence of God with the smell of sawdust and with hot summer nights. And we will always long for the "good old days" when we met with

the Lord under the nighttime sky. Nothing will ever be able to equal or replace that experience as it grows to epic proportions in our minds.

"We want to go back to those times," many Christians say. "They were wonderful."

"Well, exactly how far back do you want to go?" I would ask. Why stop with the tent and the sawdust? Go back a little farther and you can drive to the tent in a horse-drawn carriage. Better yet, go back a little farther than that and you can place guards around the tent to watch for Indians while you kneel in the sawdust to pray. Go back still farther and you will reach a time when women couldn't even enter the tent. In fact, they had to live outside the camp one week out of every month. And if you'll keep going back, you can enjoy a time when God's people wore fig leaves to the tent.

Hey, if you want to go back, then let's really go back. If you want to live in the past, then let's really live in the past. But I'm here to tell you that today is always better than yesterday, and tomorrow always has the potential to be better than today. And that's the truth! So appreciate the past, learn from the past, draw from the past, and celebrate the past. But live in the here and now, and look forward to the future. Even God got tired of standing still, so he told Moses and Israelites, *"You have made your way around this hill country long enough; now turn north"* (see Deuteronomy 2:3).

Sixth, enjoy change.

This is another indicator of whether you are young or old. The person who cannot change is the person who is "old." The person who can adapt to changing circumstances is the person who still has a lot of life to live. As Mrs. Gump (Sally Field) so often said, "Life is like a box of chocolates; you never know what you're gonna get."

So let a childlike expectancy of tomorrow grip you and lift your spirit as you get excited about the never-ending adventure of living. Don't be like the dinosaur, who resisted change and became extinct. Don't be like the movie rental companies, who refused to adapt to the worldwide web and went out of business. Instead, modify, adjust, alter, amend, revise, rework, and do something different. But even as you embrace the natural changes that are thrown at you by government, by science, and by culture, also embrace the fact that the state of your spiritual life is destined to change, as well. If you are currently living under God's abundant favor and blessing, rest assured that he is strengthening you for the mission or the battle that lies ahead. And if you are currently enduring hardship and suffering that are almost unbearable, rest in the knowledge that "this too shall pass." He will bring you *through the valley of the shadow of death*" (Psalm 23:4, emphasis mine), not "into the valley of the shadow of death" to remain there forever.

When you move beyond fear to the place of faith where God wants all of us to dwell, you will be free to be everything God created you to be and to achieve everything God created you to do. You will be happy. You will be content. You will "be strong in the Lord, and in the power of his might" (Ephesians 6:10). And your spirit will rise as you realize that God is with you and will sustain you in your difficulties while he brings you through them triumphantly.

Change is your ally and your friend. Change is a form of God's blessing in your life. When the seasons change, the leaves may change with them, but the roots of your life will grow deeper and the fruit will become sweet and ripe. Nothing can make you grow quite like change, and nothing can lift your spirit quite like the wise embrace of the changing seasons. So adapt and grow; change and thrive.

MODULE 7

SEASONS CHANGE

SEASONS CHANGE

1. What is your favorite season of the year? What changes mark this season for you? Why do you enjoy the changes that this season brings?

_____

_____

_____

2. The story goes that an ancient king had a ring designed for him that would help him maintain emotional balance in any situation. The ring was inscribed with the phrase, "This too shall pass." If you were to design a ring for yourself that would help you maintain emotional balance in your life, what would be the inscription on your ring?

_____

_____

_____

3. Some trees, like the palm, bend in the wind. Other trees, like the pine, have little flexibility. What kind of tree stands as a monument to your temperament?

_____

_____

_____

4. Change is inevitable, change is ceaseless, and change is a combination of both good and bad elements. How has change been good in your life? How has it been a negative force? From your perspective, has change been mostly good or mostly bad for you?

_____

_____

_____

5. If you are married, how did you meet your mate? If you are single, how do you plan to meet new people? Do today's methods of social interaction represent a change from the way you socialized when you were younger?

_____

_____

_____

6. Exactly one year ago today, what was the biggest problem in your life? What was the problem that consumed most of your time and attention? What has happened to that problem over the past twelve months? What does this tell you about problems and the way you should deal with them?

_____

_____

_____

7. Do you tend to be primarily past oriented, present oriented, or future oriented? How does this disposition serve you? How does it hinder you?

_____

_____

_____

8. Are you "old"? Do you adapt to change easily, or do you tend to resist change with all your might? Have you always been this way, or can you recognize a shift in your attitude over the years?

_____

_____

_____

9. Is your life currently marked by a season of testing or a season of favor? What does this tell you about God's plans for your immediate future?

_____

_____

_____

10. When the seasons become harsh, the tree tends to grow stronger and to send its roots deeper into the soil. How do the difficult seasons of life affect you? Why?

_____

_____

_____

DIGGING DEEPER

Christine Martin explains how some people develop one-year, five-year, or ten-year plans for their lives. And some people plan even farther into the future.

Do you have a long-term plan for your life? How far into the future does it extend? How specific is your plan?

_____

_____

_____

How do you balance your long-term plans with your short-term needs and the immediate circumstances of your life?

_____

_____

_____

LONG ENOUGH

You have made your way around this hill country
long enough; now turn north.
Deuteronomy 2:3

A lot of the book of Deuteronomy is a rehash of the history of Israel's forty years in the wilderness. In fact, this particular verse is found in a context where Moses is reviewing Israel's history with the people. And in reading through this recitation of Jewish history, two things become apparent.

First, God blesses action and faith. The people of Israel seemed to want to just sit back and let God do everything for them. But that's not the way God works. He works through our efforts. We have to do something. Before the people could move forward, God required them to fight foreign armies. He required them to gather manna every morning. He required them to build the Lord's tabernacle. He required them to struggle and endure the hardships of the wilderness. God would not do these things for them.

Too many people have a mistaken concept of the Christian life. They even have a mistaken concept of Heaven. Too many people believe that God is supposed to do everything for us while we just sit on our rears and criticize his efforts (like the Jews did in the wilderness). But God works through our hands. He speaks through our lips. He fights for us when we fight for ourselves. He works for us when we work for ourselves. God blesses activity, not inactivity. He blesses effort, not whining and complaining. Faith is demonstrated through action.

Second, life is perpetual motion. The thing that really shines through the biblical reconstruction of the wilderness wanderings is that each day brought something new for God's people. While the problems of the past (the Egyptian army) were now lying at the bottom of the sea, the blessings of the past (the great food of Egypt) were also gone and forgotten. At the same time, however, the pleasures of the future loomed larger in the eyes of the faithful members of the community than the delights they had been forced to surrender when they turned loose of the past.

God wants us to march forward, not stand still. He wants us to move into the future, not cling to the past. Where are you right now in your life? Have you been there "long enough?" If so, move on. You may have some battles to fight and some work to do, but God will be with you. And the Promised Land of tomorrow will be better than the wilderness you enjoy today.

SOMETHING TO THINK ABOUT

Change occurs consistently and affects every aspect of culture and every dimension of one's life. But these changes occur slowly enough that we can learn how to accommodate them. Consequently, we sometimes fail to even notice them.

Over the course of your life, what are the biggest and most impressive changes you have witnessed in the world of technology?

_____

_____

Over the course of your life, what are the most conse-
quential changes you have observed in society?

_____

_____

_____

Since you were born, what are the biggest political
changes you have noticed in your country and the world?

_____

_____

_____

MY PRAYER FOR ADAPTABILITY

Father, creation itself teaches me the importance and the
necessity of being able to change. Those things in the world
that have not been able to change have eventually perished.
But those things in the world that have been able to change
have endured. So I ask you to teach me how to change and
how to accept the changes that are taking place around me.
There are some things I should never change in my life. Help
me to never wander from you. But I need to change myself,
and I need to adapt to the changes in my world so I can relate
to those around me and be an effective mouthpiece for you.
I also need to change so I can extract all the pleasure from
life that you intended me to know. So help me to bend with

the winds of change. Even though I do not want to change in my moral composition, I do want to change in my ability to relate to my world. In Jesus' name, Amen!

MY SPIRITUAL JOURNAL

Take a few moments to record your thoughts regarding this week's session on changing seasons. What new things did you learn? What new insights and revelations have you had? What life-changing truths did Christine Martin impart that have impacted your thinking? What changes will you make in the days ahead?

FOOD FOR THOUGHT

The Bible describes God's Words as spiritual bread and spiritual meat. It is designed to nourish the spirit and the soul in the same way that food nourishes the body. So read the following scripture every day this week, repeating it out loud when you read it, and memorize it, if possible. And while you meditate upon this passage, make notes about anything you may observe about your personal life and any changes you may want to make.

To every thing there is a season, and a time to every purpose under heaven: a time to be born, and a time to die; a time

to plant, and a time to pluck up that which is planted; a time to kill, and a time to heal; a time to break down, and a time to build up; a time to weep, and a time to laugh; a time to mourn, and a time to dance; a time to cast away stones, and a time to gather stones together; a time to embrace, and a time to refrain from embracing; a time to get, and a time to lose; a time to keep, and a time to cast away; a time to rend, and a time to sew; a time to keep silence, and a time to speak; a time to love, and a time to hate; a time of war, and a time of peace"
Ecclesiastes 3:1-8 (KJV)

_____

_____

_____

WISDOM FROM ABOVE

The righteous will flourish like a palm tree, they will grow like a cedar of Lebanon.
Psalm 92:12

To him who overcomes, I will give some of the hidden manna. I will also give him a white stone with a new name written on it, known only to him who receives it.
Revelation 2:17

Yea, though I walk through the valley of the shadow of death, I will fear no evil: for thou art with me; thy rod and thy staff they comfort me.
Psalm 23:4 (KJV)

COULD YOU REPEAT THAT?

Change is inevitable, but misery is optional.

If you want to survive to embrace the future, you have to release the past.

When you just can't enjoy anything that is different or new because you are trapped in the things that are comfortable and old, you are not growing; you are dying.

IN A NUTSHELL

If you don't like change, you might want to relocate to a different planet.

CHAPTER 8:

Get Your Directions from Upstairs

When all is said and done, you must know in your heart that your direction comes from the Lord. If it does, all will be well in your life. If it does not, chaos surely looms.

If you are a Christian, you have experienced God's leading before. You are familiar with his inner voice. You also know that there is a joy and tranquility that comes to lift your spirit when you know you are precisely where God wants you to be, doing what he wants you to do. So open your heart's door and allow your spirit to be elevated as you surrender yourself to the will of God. He knows your thoughts anyway, so you might as well let him in. And he knows the plans you have for your life, so you might as well share those plans with him and let him share with you the things he sees for your future. Remember, God created you, so he knows exactly where you should be heading and exactly what you need in order to get there. So what are you waiting for? Develop a healthy relationship with God and get his direction for your life.

Some people struggle all their lives to hear the voice of God and to understand God's direction for their lives. But getting direction from God is actually easy. In fact, it's not complicated at all. Nevertheless, many of us make it complicated or we make excuses as to why we cannot hear from the Lord.

Nevertheless, divine direction is imperative for the believer and absolutely essential for the person who desires to walk in God's will and to live under the favor and protection of the Almighty. Without God's direction, we are lost without a compass. We are floating helplessly on the open seas, totally at the mercy of the forces of nature and totally incapable of steering the ship of our own lives.

It doesn't take us long to figure out that life is difficult and that the course is dangerous. Without God's guidance, we make more mistakes than we would like, and we do more damage than we would like. So we start longing for direction from above. For those among us who believe in God, we know that he is the source of all wisdom and we know that he holds the future in his hands. So we turn to him, and we try to hear his voice and to differentiate that voice from all the other voices that vie for our attention in this world.

But for those among us who do not believe in God or have an intimate relationship with him, we look elsewhere. We look to horoscopes. We look to Ouija boards. We look to therapists or consultants or to friends we would like to emulate. Unfortunately, these voices, like the other voices of guidance in the world, typically lead us astray and their wisdom is hit or miss. Over time, therefore, we come to appreciate and long for the direction that only God can provide.

And this makes perfect sense. When you need to go somewhere you have never been before, don't you usually get directions? If you are going to a job interview, for instance, or to a new mall or a new restaurant, don't you typically write down the directions before you leave home or access your GPS once you realize you don't know where you're going?

Learn to the do the same thing with God. Stop and ask directions, and the way you feel about your life will change. Don't make excuses any longer. Just do it! Don't give the same old excuses that you don't have time, that you're too busy, that your children need your attention, that your boss or husband won't give you the space, or that you have deadlines or responsibilities hanging over your head. Make the time to spend time with the Lord, and you will soon learn to hear his voice for yourself. You will soon learn to know his wisdom and to yield to it.

It's that easy. Really! Just talk to God. If you would get in the habit of spending a little bit of time every day talking to God, your life would turn around quickly, because he would become a very present friend and a voice of reason in the midst of chaos. He would become an anchor and a shield for you. He would become involved in the details of your life and would become the centerpiece of your daily decisions.

Great people are decisive. They're not impulsive, but they are decisive. And they are decisive because they know how to quickly gather the facts, weigh them, and then move forward with determination, never looking back or second-guessing their choices. This is why so many great people throughout history had a reputation for believing in God and spending time with him in prayer. People who seem to have direction for their lives often get that direction by spending time with the Lord. Even the busiest people pray.

David was like this. David was a great man, and he was a great leader. In fact, no other figure in biblical history was more highly exalted than David. David was a simple shepherd boy from a humble family. He had no formal education and no great achievements to his name. Yet he became the greatest king in Israel's history, and he became the architect of God's temple and the mastermind behind the worship services that would take place within it. He also was the benefactor of an everlasting covenant with God, and his kingdom has been established forever. Even the Son of God himself was known as the "Son of David" (Luke 18:38). But David's great success was based partly on the fact that David didn't know everything, and he realized that he didn't know everything. So he would routinely seek the will of God and the direction of the Lord for his life.

In David's time, believing people received God's guidance differently than they do today. Today, we learn to pray and to hear God's voice in our hearts through the direct witness of God's Spirit. But in David's day, the Holy Spirit had not yet been poured out upon humanity, so people did not have a sense of the abiding presence of God. They had to discern God's will in a different way. And the way they did it was quite strange. Let me explain.

When God established the law that became the moral and legal code for the nation of Israel, he communicated that law through his servant Moses. But a large part of the Jewish law consisted of a lot of intricate details regarding the design of the tabernacle, the garments for the priesthood, and the many details regarding the way to prepare sacrifices and offerings and observe the feasts and celebrations that connected the Jewish people as a nation.

I don't want to go into a lot of detail here about the Law of Moses. You can find all of it woven throughout the books of Exodus, Leviticus, and Numbers, and you can read a condensed version of it in Deuteronomy. But the thing I want to focus on here is the design of the high priest's garments, specifically a piece of the high priest's wardrobe that was known as the "ephod."

The ephod was a breastplate of some sort that the high priest wore over his other garments, kind of like a fancy vest. It was made of gold, blue, purple, scarlet, and fine twined linen. According to The New Unger's Bible Dictionary, the ephod "fit closely around the shoulders and was held on by two straps." And on top of each of the shoulder straps, there was an onyx stone encased in a filigree setting of gold that was engraved with the names of six of the tribes of Israel.

Over the ephod, the high priest wore a "breastpiece." The breastpiece was a square piece of cloth made of the same material as the ephod and worn on top of the ephod, on the chest of the high priest. In this breastpiece were twelve precious stones set in gold and arranged in four rows of three. A name of one of the twelve tribes of Israel was engraved on each stone.

On the breastpiece was a pocket that held two mysterious items called the Urim and the Thummim. Nobody knows for sure what these two items were or what they were made of. Even early historians like Josephus and Philo were uncertain regarding the nature of these two small objects. What is known, however, is that the Urim and the Thummim were separate from the breastpiece itself. They had to be inserted into the pocket of the breastpiece after the high priest had attached the breastpiece to the ephod. We also know that these two objects were used in some way to ascertain the will of God. Some people believe the Urim and the Thummim were similar to two dice. By "casting" them, the high priest could determine God's will by obtaining the Lord's response to a specific question.

The exact nature of the Urim and the Thummim and

how they were used remains a mystery to this day, and the mere fact that they existed is one of the most amazing facts in the Bible. But the point here is that David made use of these mysterious objects. Because God had given the Urim and the Thummim to the high priest to help the Israelites understand the will of God, David took advantage of this precious resource. Throughout his adult life, he stayed in close contact with the high priest and often instructed the high priest to seek God's will on his behalf by using the Urim and the Thummim.

God was impressed with David because of David's relentless pursuit of God's will. Perhaps that is why God described David as *"a man after my own heart"* (Acts 13:22). God favored David all his life because of David's high regard for the will of God. But God removed King Saul from the throne of Israel and allowed him to die a premature and humiliating death, partly because Saul "did not inquire of the Lord" (I Chronicles 10:14). In other words, Saul seldom utilized the precious Urim and Thummim that were available to him. Like so many modern believers, he didn't think it was important to know the will of God regarding the daily matters of his life. So he never devoted the necessary time to seeking God's will or understanding it. But David made God's will his highest priority.

God cannot communicate with you about your life if your ignore him. So don't complain about his lack of involvement in your life if you don't do your part to keep the lines of communication open. Do you want to live happy? Do you want to live free? Do you want to have joy? Do you want to have peace? Then talk to the Lord. It's that simple! It's not complicated; it just takes some effort and a little discipline.

When Jesus was on this earth and he was traveling from village to village, healing sicknesses and teaching the people about God, he attracted to him a small group of men who eventually became the leaders of his fledgling church following his resurrection and ascension. These men—Peter, James, John, Bartholomew, Nathanael, Thomas, and others—were "ordinary men." In fact, the Bible uses that exact phrase to describe them (see Acts 4:13). They were fishermen, businessmen, and tax collectors. None of them were highly educated. None of them came from noble stock. And none of them were particularly gifted in any aspect of life.

Nevertheless, in spite of their humble origins, these eleven men shook the world and reshaped human history. The impact of their lives is still felt today by the majority of the world's people. But what made these men so great? What transformed them? What enabled them to move beyond their "ordinary" status to their eventual status of notoriety and fame? What made them great?

It was the time they spent with the Lord. In fact, even their most ardent opponents realized that this was true. The members of the Sanhedrin, the Jewish council of religious leaders who contended for the traditional Jewish faith and who opposed the emerging church with maniacal zeal, interviewed these men *"and realized that they were unschooled, ordinary men"* who *"had been with Jesus"* (Acts 4:13).

You, too, can be completely transformed. You, too, can transition from "ordinary" to "great." Like the apostles of Jesus, you can be directed daily by the Spirit of God. You can hear the voice of God within your own heart, and you can live your life with an elevated spirit. But you have to talk to God if you want these things to happen. You have to hear from him. And you have to spend time with him if you want to hear from him.

If you feel weak, give God a try. If you feel down in the dumps, give God a try. If you feel "ordinary" or mediocre or defeated or just plain lost, give God a try. After all, what do you have to lose? Remember, God can see the future. But you can't. He knows no lack, no oppression, and no doubt. But you do. So if you're smart, you will stop acting like Saul, who thought he could handle life on his own and ended up losing the throne and his life. Or you can be like David, who realized that he had the greatest imaginable resource at his disposal—the wisdom and knowledge of God—and who decided that he was going to tap into that inexhaustible resource.

All of us have to make decisions regarding the future direction of our lives, but none of us live in the future. You and I and every other person on earth live in the "here and now." What we really need is another Urim and Thummim.

We need some way to peer into the future and to know what is going to happen. As we ponder our options, we need to know what will happen if we make this decision and what will happen if we make the other one instead.

But we can't do that. Human beings are finite creatures. We are confined by space, and we are confined by time. But fortunately for us, God has no such limitations. He lives in the past, the present, and the future simultaneously.

You and I are like those spectators who watch the Macy's Thanksgiving Day Parade from ground level. We can only see what is happening right in front of us. We cannot see the bands and the floats that have already passed, and we cannot see the giant balloons and Santa's sleigh, which have not yet arrived. We can only see what is taking place right in front of our eyes at this precise moment in time.

But God is like the billionaire executive, who watches the parade from his penthouse office, high atop Manhattan. He is like the important dignitary who watches from the Goodyear Blimp. God can see the entire parade simultaneously. While he is looking down upon the grand marshal at the front of the parade route, he can see Santa Claus trailing up the rear. He can see yesterday, today, and tomorrow all at the same time.

So doesn't it make sense, if we need direction, to tap into God's limitless knowledge and his wisdom? Obviously, he's not going to show us everything about the future, and he is not going to answer all our silly questions. He is not a Ouija board, and he did not give us the gift of prayer so we could know who will win the Super Bowl this coming February. But when it comes to the important matters of our individual lives and when it comes to right living and morality and the important decisions that can shape our destinies, God is more than interested in sharing his insights with us. Wouldn't it be great if we had a similar interest in obtaining those insights?

Learn to talk to God, and learn to talk to him as a friend (see James 2:23). He's not interested in your fancy speech, because you won't be auditioning for the Senate chaplaincy. He's not interested in your religious rituals, because you won't be coronating a pope. God just wants you to open your mouth and talk to him the same way you would talk to your mom, your dad, your husband, your wife, or even your closest friend. Just have a daily chat with him.

But before you do, let me give you one piece of advice that can make your time with the Lord more meaningful and more productive: Clean up before you enter God's presence. What do I mean by "clean up"?

If you had a special meeting with an important person or if you had a significant interview that could change the course of your life, wouldn't you get ready before going to that meeting or that interview? Ladies, wouldn't you wash your hair, put on some makeup, and wear your nicest clothes? Guys, wouldn't you shave, take a shower, and at least try to match your shirt and tie? Of course you would! You wouldn't just roll out of bed and go to an important meeting in your pajamas.

You should regard your time with the Lord similarly. To obtain God's direction for your life as you try to deal with the many changes that are taking place inside you and all around you, you need to spend some time with him every day. You need to visit with the one who made you and understands you better than you understand yourself.

But before you go to that meeting, you need to prepare yourself for it. You need to decide that you want certain things to be different in your life. You need to prepare yourself to receive wisdom from somebody who knows a lot more than you know. You need to adopt an attitude of humility that will enable you to hear God's voice and respond to it, even though the actions he directs you to take might lead to short-term discomfort. You need to be teachable, not obstinate. You need to be worshipful, not defiant. And you need to possess a thankful heart for the things God has already done in your life.

God is waiting. So shut the door, turn off the phone, put the dog in the other room, and talk to God. If you want something you've never had, you're going to have to do something you've never done. All the power to change is in your hands.

The ability to lift your spirit is simply the ability to take action in order to make a few vital things happen in your life.

As I sign off, I want to encourage you to make some time to talk to the person who knows everything you need to know and who can impart to you all the wisdom, all the patience, and all the fortitude you could possibly need to go from where you are to where you want to be. I also want to encourage you to meditate on the things he whispers to your heart and the things he has written to you in his best-selling book, the Bible. And finally I want to encourage you to take action by taking baby steps to implement the things he is telling you do. If you do your part, he will do his part. And soon, you will see your spirit rise. You will see growth and change that will encourage your heart and infuse new vitality into every aspect of your life.

You can do this, because I have done this. So just make the decision and go for it. And remember that God will be with you and he will help you, because the changes you want to make are the changes God wants you to make. Those changes are a good thing, not a bad thing. They're a God-thing, not a human thing. So lean on the Lord, and you will succeed, and your satisfaction will rise with every step you take and with every battle you win. Your spirit will rise too, and your life will completely change.

MODULE 8

GET YOUR DIRECTIONS FROM UPSTAIRS

GET YOUR DIRECTIONS FROM UPSTAIRS

1. Describe the sense of joy that you have felt in the past when you knew God had spoken to your heart to give you specific direction in an important matter.

_____

_____

_____

2. Do you struggle to hear the voice of God in your own heart? Do you struggle to differentiate his voice from your own selfish desires or from the voices of all the "advisors" who surround you? How can you tell the difference between God's voice and the other voices that vie for your attention?

_____

_____

_____

3. Christine Martin describes some of the alternative sources of guidance that people employ when they cannot or will not hear the voice of God. People rely on horoscopes, therapists, and close friends, for instance. To what alternative sources have you fled in the past for your own guidance and direction?

_____

_____

_____

4. Some people claim they don't have enough time to talk to God. Others claim that their children or their spouses need their attention. And still others claim that life's responsibilities must come first. What excuse do you sometimes use to justify the lack of time you devote to the Lord?

_____

_____

_____

5. In your opinion, why did God regard David so highly and elevate him before his peers?

_____

_____

_____

6. Why do you think King Saul refused to consult the Lord for guidance when God's guidance was so readily available to him?

_____

_____

_____

7. Has God helped you to make the transition from "ordinary" to "great" in certain aspects of your life? Explain.

_____

_____

_____

8. What is the most serious matter confronting you right now that requires the wisdom and guidance of God?

_____

_____

_____

9. In your opinion, if God was so meticulous regarding the precise construction of the tabernacle and the precise construction of the high priest's garments, why is he disinterested in our pomp and ceremony when it comes to our time with him?

_____

_____

_____

10. What do you need to do personally to "clean up" prior to your daily meeting with God?

_____

_____

_____

DIGGING DEEPER

According to Christine Martin, it doesn't take long to figure out that life is difficult and that the course is dangerous. Without God's guidance, we can make more mistakes in life than we would like, and we can do more damage than we would like.

In your opinion, what is the biggest mistake you have ever made that you wish you could reverse?

_____

_____

_____

What damages resulted from your inability to adequately predict the outcome of this bad situation?

_____

_____

_____

IT'S IN THE FACE

> *Look to the LORD and his strength;*
> *seek his face always.*
> *I Chronicles 16:11*

For just a moment, think about the people you love. Picture them in your mind. When you picture them, what do you see? You see their faces. In fact, you may possibly carry pictures of your loved ones with you. If you do, you carry pictures of their faces. Nobody has ever walked into another person's home to see a family portrait of eight knees hanging over the living room mantle. Instead, the mantle will be adorned with a family portrait of four faces.

A person's identity is in his face. A person's face is usually the first thing we notice about the person. A person's face is the thing we use to distinguish that person from all the other people we know. A person's face is the focus of our attention when we talk to him or her. The face is the expressive vehicle of our human emotions.

God wants us to seek his face. In other words, he wants us to know him personally. He wants us to draw close to him and get to know him in an intimate way. He wants to have a close and abiding relationship with us. He wants to be a friend, as well as our heavenly father.

Deep and abiding friendships don't just happen by accident. They happen because the two individuals involved deliberately seek out one another's company because both parties are enhanced by the relationship. When they are together, both are fulfilled and both are satisfied.

So seek the Lord. Set aside some time to spend with him every day. At first, this will take discipline and effort. In time, it will become a habit. And soon after that, it will become an integral part of your life that you cannot live without. It will be highly meaningful and extremely important. And your relationship with God will blossom.

SOMETHING TO THINK ABOUT

Many voices compete for our attention and submission. In fact, most people reject God's guidance for their lives and turn to other forms of counsel.

Have you ever consulted a horoscope for direction? What was your experience? Why do you think so many people put confidence in the newspaper horoscope?

_____

_____

_____

Therapy is an effective form of treatment for many psychological disorders and traumas, but some people have described the modern therapist as "the high priest of the humanist movement." Where do you believe Christians should draw the line in their acceptance of therapy as a viable form of assistance in their lives?

_____

_____

_____

Do your friends ever try to advise you? How do they react if you reject their counsel in favor of God's guidance from within?

_____

_____

_____

MY PRAYER FOR SPIRITUAL INTIMACY

Father, forgive me for neglecting you. If the people I loved the most neglected me, I would be devastated. Yet I have neglected you. I call on you when I need you, but I don't spend the time with you that is necessary for really getting to know you. Now I'm in a bit of a trap, because I have built my life around a schedule that doesn't involve you, at least not at the level that I need. So please help me. I want to be with you, and I want to know you. I want to make you a vital part of every aspect of my life, and I want to hear your voice so you can guide me through the maze of life. So help me set aside the time, and help me make good use of that time. Help me talk to you as I would talk to a friend. And let me hear your voice respond to me. In Jesus' name, Amen!

MY SPIRITUAL JOURNAL

Take a few moments to record your thoughts regarding this week's session on hearing God's voice and receiving God's direction. What new things did you learn? What new insights and revelations have you had? What life-changing truths did Christine Martin impart that have impacted your thinking? What changes will you make in the days ahead?

_____

_____

_____

FOOD FOR THOUGHT

The Bible describes God's Words as spiritual bread and spiritual meat. It is designed to nourish the spirit and the soul in the same way that food nourishes the body. So read the following scripture every day this week, repeating it out loud when you read it, and memorize it, if possible. And while you meditate upon this passage, make notes about anything you may observe about your personal life and any changes you may want to make.

Now the Philistines had come and raided the Valley of Rephaim; so David inquired of God: *"Shall I go and attack the Philistines? Will you hand them over to me?"* The LORD answered him, *"Go, I will hand them over to you."* So David and his men went up to Baal Perazim, and there he defeated them. He said, *"As waters break out, God has broken out against my enemies by my hand."* So that place was called Baal Perazim.

I Chronicles 14:9-11

_____

_____

_____

WISDOM FROM ABOVE

When they saw the courage of Peter and John and realized that they were unschooled, ordinary men, they were astonished and they took note that these men had been with Jesus.
Acts 4:13

I have found David son of Jesse a man after my own heart; he will do everything I want him to do.
Acts 13:22

And the scripture was fulfilled that says, "Abraham believed God, and it was credited to him as righteousness," and he was called God's friend.
James 2:23

COULD YOU REPEAT THAT?

When all is said and done, you must know in your heart that your direction comes from the Lord.

Without God's direction, we are lost without a compass.

God cannot communicate with you about your life if you ignore him.

IN A NUTSHELL

If you want something you've never had, you're going to have to do something you've never done.

CAN I INTRODUCE YOU TO MY BEST FRIEND?

Before you lay this book aside, make sure you put God first so that you can walk in His Favor, Blessings, and Increase and have the desires of your heart.

First, ask Jesus to cleanse you of your sins. You do not have to clean up your life first—God will do that for you. He will also give you a new heart, new desires, and the Spirit of Truth.

If you truly want a change in your life, then pray this prayer out loud and believe:

"Father in Heaven, I've heard Your Word, and I want to be born again. Jesus, cleanse me of my sins. I want to be a child of God. I want to give my life to You. Make me a new person. Be my Lord and Savior.

I believe I'm now born again, because the Word of God says I am! Jesus is my Lord. Thank you, Jesus, for a new life. Amen!"

Now do not go by what you feel. Go by what God's Word says. You are saved—you are born again. Believe it!

WE WANT TO HEAR FROM YOU!

If you prayed this prayer sincerely, call us at 407.629.0015. Also, we want to hear your praise reports and testimonies of God's Favor on your life! Write to us at

DAVE AND CHRISTINE MARTIN

P.O. Box 608150 • Orlando, FL 32860

Visit Us

www.davemartin.org

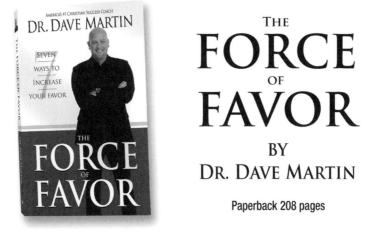

ULC ORLANDO

ULTIMATE LIFE CONFERENCE

with

Dr. Dave & Christine Martin

3 DAYS OF LEARNING, LEISURE & LAUGHTER

The Ultimate Life Conference is the Premier Christian Personal Development Conference for Business Owners, Achievers, Networkers and Kingdom Builders!

Stay Connected Online

 @ULConference

 /UltimateLifeConference

To Register & Get More Information:
WWW.ULTIMATELIFECONFERENCE.COM